RUNNING FOR SUCCESS
Overcome Low Motivation, Boost Your Mental Health, and Increase Your Productivity

ELLIS WARREN

RUNNING FOR SUCCESS

Copyright © 2020 Ellis Warren
First edition: November 2020

ellis warren
RUNNER AUTHOR

The right of ELLIS WARREN to be identified as the author of this work has been asserted by him in accordance with the Copyright, Designs and Patents Act 1988.

All rights reserved. No part of this publication may be reproduced, transmitted, or stored in a retrieval system in any form or by any means without permission in writing from the copyright owner, nor otherwise circulated in any form of binding or cover other than that in which it is published and without a similar condition being imposed on the subsequent purchaser.

For inquiries, please direct all email correspondence to:
ejameswarren@gmail.com

ISBN: 979-8-69434-133-2

www.EllisWarren.com
Book Cover by Ellis Warren
Cover Photo by MarathonFoto

To everyone who has supported me

Contents

Introduction   1

Part One: Lift-off

Chapter 1
It starts with a choice   7

Chapter 2
Finding your inspirations   21

Chapter 3
Your first run is no one else's business   39

Chapter 4
The early euphoria of running   57

Part Two: Lessons

Chapter 5
The one mistake every new runner makes   77

Chapter 6
Injuries: Learn your lessons   95

Chapter 7
Willpower: The key to sustained success   113

Part Three: Merits

Chapter 8
How to run for charity and why you'll love it	133

Chapter 9
The first event: An unforgettable experience	151

Chapter 10
The runner's life	175

Chapter 11
Marathon day: No challenge greater	193

Chapter 12
Post-marathon: What you should be aware of	215

Chapter 13
Onto the next challenge	229

Acknowledgements

I would like to first thank all of those who very kindly read early chapter drafts, offered their feedback, and helped ensure this book made it across the line: Lesley Wright, Joe de Souza, Callum Barrett, Oly Newton (@Run4YourMind), Joe Cutts (@RunningwithJoe), Bertie Robertson, Autumn Stenhouse, and Darya Maryam. Your encouraging and insightful comments really helped me through the daunting process of writing a book for the first time, so I thank you all.

A huge thanks goes to Emma Kirk Martin- thank you for always telling me how it is and encouraging me to improve as a writer. Look out for Emma everyone, she's immensely talented and I'm hugely excited for her first release.

A genuine thank you to Morning Musume- we will probably never meet, but the impact you had during my first year of university was ridiculously profound.

A massive shout out to Mum, James, Nan, and Merlot. Thank you for the support and putting up with me during these difficult lockdown months.

Ayano, Ayumi, and Mako, my dearest friends in Osaka- thank you for the days burning bright red at the beach, the evenings belting out our classics down karaoke mics, and the crazy nights dancing until dawn. Just a few of the many unforgettable memories together. I can't wait for our adventures to continue.

To the Goda family- my Japanese family! My gratitude for always taking care of me in Kobe. Our times together were some of my favourite memories from a very special year. Additionally, I would like to extend my gratitude to the Takemoto family and the Uyama family for their amazing kindness and generosity, and also thank the Kobe University Marathon Club for warmly welcoming me into their group- I will always cherish that summer together and am grateful for the opportunity.

A big thanks to Ethan, Gianni, Matt, Brandon, Rob, and Blaze- always there for me, never failing to make me crease. You boys are the best mates I could ever ask for and I love you all to bits.

And finally, my sincerest gratitude to everyone who donated and supported Project Run earlier this year. Together, we raised over £1,750 for Mind during a time when the nation's mental health was undergoing stresses like never before. Together we did something great and I will forever be grateful for your support and generous contributions.

All my love, and I hope you enjoy my first book.

- Ellis
October 2020

'If you're going to face a challenge it has to be a real challenge. You can't accomplish anything without the possibility of failure.'

— Lazarus Lake

Introduction

This book chronicles the story of how running changed my life. It is a story about succeeding through goal setting, overcoming challenges, and seeing progress through a long-term lens.

Running is important because it reveals our true character. It shows us how we react to setbacks and situations where success is not easy to obtain nor guaranteed. I genuinely believe anyone can run a marathon, but does everyone try? Does everyone have the patience, tenacity, and vision to train for months and then complete 26.2 miles? The determining factor is always mindset.

Training for a marathon is compatible with the process of working towards any worthwhile goal, i.e. a mammoth task coupled with numerous mental setbacks that may include doubt, depression, and anxiety. There are always external and internal barriers to success. Therefore, as you read this book, realise that the marathon journey is relatable to any goal-oriented endeavour. The lessons here are not just limited to running.

This book is for anyone who wants to make a change in their lives. It for anyone who has struggled with motivation and the mental warfare that we battle on our paths to success. It is for anyone looking to overcome a daunting and overwhelming situation, whether that be a marathon, university, exams, a job, or a completely new environment.

I have written this book to provide a genuine example of how becoming a runner can help you reach the best physical shape of your life, and enhance your mindset to explore capabilities and unprecedented levels of ambition you may not have thought possible. I will tell the story of my first marathon, featuring the many lessons I learnt along the way on how to run for success without falling into the many traps that cause so many to quit.

The central proposition to this winning mindset is willpower, which teaches us to refuse becoming a slave to the volatile and unreliable nature of motivation, and instead encourages us to liberate ourselves from doubtful thoughts and feelings by choosing to take action. Willpower pushes us to ditch our ego, excuses, and laziness, and ensures we honour the commitments we make to ourselves and carry out each goal to the finish.

Running is one of the main ways to build willpower because of the mental discipline required to be successful at it. Once you build willpower and learn how to use it, the benefits will branch out into other aspects of your life, pushing you to strive and persevere through each and every goal you set.

INTRODUCTION

If running for success was easy, everyone would do it. But in reality it's hard, particularly when you encounter your first setbacks. I have therefore arranged this book into three parts to guide you through the process. The first part will help brainstorm sources of inspiration for kicking off your running routine, alongside how to set a goal to accomplish something remarkable *and* yield's the sport's maximum benefits. I will take you through my first ever run- hiccupping with a hangover but revelling in the magical euphoria that is the runner's high- and you will read of how running had an instant impact on my productivity, helping to organise my university work into achievable daily tasks.

The second part shall then document the setbacks and the inevitable problems we all encounter which cause so many to give up on their journey of self-empowerment. It is worth sticking through these because this is where you will learn the most about yourself and experience the most growth. Specifically, I will show you the exact mistakes I made when starting my marathon training and tell you how to prevent taking the full blow when things get tough. By learning the lessons early, you will be better positioned to enjoy a smoother rise to success from your running.

The third part is the longest, for it encompasses the many merits running has to offer. I will introduce running for charity- one of the highlights of my whole journey- and my very memorable first ever running event at a world-renowned Formula 1 track. All of the many benefits and breakthroughs from becoming a runner will be revealed, followed by the big day itself-my first ever marathon- I won't spoil it, but let's just say it was the worst possible day to run 26.2 miles.

Finally, as a bonus, I will heed warning to the one big trap following your success that could potentially reset you back to zero. Once aware of how to deal with this pitfall, you're set for life- you'll be ready to go out there and seize success in any area with the skills gained on your running journey.

I am definitely not an expert, but instead seek to share my experiences and lessons which I believe may be encouraging and beneficial to those who are in a similar position to when I decided to start running.

My story is just one of many and with the same tenacity, you could very well be the next tale of success. The true benefits of running have gone unknown for too long; I hope that by sharing the wonders of running and willpower, you too can enjoy a happier, healthier, and more prosperous life. You've already taken your first step in picking up this book, so welcome to the club- think big and challenge bold, for today you start breaking barriers.

Part One: Lift-off

Chapter 1
It starts with a choice

I used to think of myself as a real loser.

Let's paint the scene: it's November 2016 and I'm two months into my first term at university. Lectures have finished after another mild autumn day, where soggy brown leaves line the streets. The sun had long disappeared before my economics class wrapped up early and so it would be another solitary walk back to halls with my headphones on full volume, blasting pure dissonance through my already aching head.

I return home pacing through reception with my head down, turning right out of the courtyard into my ground floor flat. Inside, I dash into the kitchen to heat up a ready meal, wearing a static forced smile to acknowledge my flatmate, who is smoking so much weed she's got both extractor fans on maximum. I retreat to my room, throw my rucksack onto wherever the floor is visible and allow my body to limply collapse on top of the bed with a long sigh.

I've spoken to no one today. I have genuinely not opened my mouth once to speak.

I stare at the ceiling and think back to the glory days only four months prior, when I was still in sixth form with all my best friends, happy and laughing every day without a care in the world. At prom I was even awarded 'Happiest Person in the Year'- you wouldn't believe that now though. Now that is all in the past. Now I am a university student, living in London, or at least that's what the electoral roll should tell you. I don't quite remember why I was so set on entering university anymore, nor exactly why I continue to get out of bed each morning and attend these classes- they're all too hard for me and I'm already behind. I stare into nothingness and wonder, *why am I here? What is the point?*

Starting university was an overwhelming experience, and I wasn't coping well at all. I struggled to make friends, couldn't understand the work, and in general despised the whole 'university experience'. All I looked forward to each morning was the fact that the end of term would be one day closer.

But, six months later a remarkable turnaround had occurred. I returned home for the summer with two medals proudly dangling from my neck, top grades in all modules, and a renewed energy and vigour for life. I was a new man. This unprecedented personal revolution began on the day I decided to become a runner. From that day, I unknowingly ventured into a world far deeper, and far greater than I could have ever possibly envisioned. Within the world of running, I embarked on a journey of remarkable discoveries, both about myself and about the skills behind success.

It was also from running that I learned how to control my own mind, a mind that had started to neglect its own power and potential.

Before I joined university, running was just another form of exercise to me. I never viewed it as a sport with much attraction to my demographic; girls don't exactly come chasing after you if you tell them you're a runner, they might even think you've got commitment issues. Runners, in general, never seem to get the star status of footballers. In school, the coolest kids were on the football team while in the cross country, the skinniest kids were often signed up to compete based purely on natural selection. Or, if you had a certain type of humour like at my school, you'd sign up the fat kids and watch them bounce off each other like Beyblades for three miles.

Running never struck me with the envy factor you get when you see a footballer curl one into the top corner and celebrate in front of thousands of fans. Well, not from an outside perspective it didn't. But- and this is a huge But- my perspective changed drastically when I became a runner myself. Now, every time I see a runner, I'm struck with either a rush of envy that they're running and I'm not, or the borderline irresistible urge to catch up and inform them, 'I also went for a run today y'know!'

You see, runners go much of their entire lives as the unsung heroes. But they don't care, because they know something that non-runners don't. They know from first-hand experience the phenomenal benefits, both physical and mental, that a simple run can offer. They know of the emphatic ways running can shape ordinary bodies and minds into something extraordinary. They know that magic truly exists in the form of the 'runner's high'.

The magic of running is like a secret, but it really shouldn't be. You have to try it yourself to truly understand its benefits. That's why most people on this planet are still oblivious to the one sure change in their lifestyle that could spark a personal revolution. Reading this book alone won't be enough to give you a full insight into how amazing running can be, but it will show you just one example of how it can equip you to combat life's negativities and struggles, and push you into becoming something greater.

This is my coming of age story where running changed it all. This is the story of how running sent my grades soaring at university, turned me from boy to man, and perhaps most important of all, gave me a mindset primed for success ahead of any challenge I dare undertake in life. It may sound a bit Hollywood, but it's a story that so many live to tell, because each and every one of us is capable of making this remarkable leap into greatness. You could be next.

The turnaround was fast and drastic- within 5 months I had become a completely new person. I owe this mainly to the greatest skill running has taught me so far: willpower. Willpower is a skill transferable to many areas of our working lives. In the long term, willpower will push you beyond the limits of motivation- our most unreliable driver- and push you to see each task through to its end. It will also serve as the great regulator in the inevitable struggles coupled with difficult endeavours. Willpower functions beyond low moods and motivation- it makes us get stuff done.

Woeful Warren

Allow me to humour you with my woeful start to university. For anyone who has ever struggled with motivation, you may resonate with this book's themes. If you have ever struggled with low self-esteem or depression, then I hope my example of how I learnt to combat such thoughts will be of benefit to you. I'm going to first tell you about my near miss with the trench of defeatist mentality. You may or may not find it a pitiful read.

It all starts with sudden upheaval. Moving to university feels like being untimely ripped from the womb of your faithful hometown surroundings. One day, I was relocated an hour up the road to London armed with determination to get a bachelor's degree and ASDA's range of home essentials. From small towns to the capital of the world- I was leaving home (kind of) and about to get struck by the full force of the winds of change; this being London, they were weed-scented winds with the odd Big Mac box drifting along for the ride.

The first 24 hours in London were so action-packed it was like I had lived a life in a day. In the morning, my dad helped me move my belongings before we headed out to get some pie and mash by Regent's Canal. Familiar and comforting father and son time- but by the time we returned to the halls he didn't stay long after he farted in my new room and we both realised there was hardly any ventilation. He made a swift escape and left me to start a completely new life. Now I was properly on my own, unless you count the fumes.

That night, I met with one of my mates from secondary school who had joined the same university, and he bought along one of his new mates. We had decided to go to the first freshers event of the year, but the two of them were running late by an hour. In that time, I tried to boost my sociability by beginning my pre-drinking routine on an empty stomach, which obviously seemed like a good idea at the time.

Four cans of Strongbow later and I suddenly found myself in the kitchen with *all* my new flatmates. The majority of them were exchange students with one master's student and they're all sober. On this grand occasion, we were having our first 'flat meeting', where I was absolutely steaming. It was a truly dire situation- I maintained a tipsy grip on the worktop for balance and chatted some proper rubbish. I sensed awkward glances around the room as I blurted out intelligent lines such as, 'Yeah it's so great to be here in London with all the cultures innit.'

Conveniently for my flatmates, my old mate Emilio and new best mate Kibo finally arrived and carried me out to go clubbing for the night. So far, so smooth, eh? Thankfully, the whole of London was equally dizzy that evening. In the club, we befriended what felt like the entire city as we danced away to hyped up chart music. It was mad. We danced without a care in the world on stage in a massive group and at one point I discovered a white girl with dreadlocks twerking on me- *hell yeah, uni life*. I believed I had properly initiated myself into the student life by that point.

How wrong was I! Despite retaining a clear memory of my exciting night, all my new friends seemed to have had their memories wiped the next morning. False start.

The start of my *actual* university life was- to put it lightly- a nightmare. I caught the infamous 'freshers flu' after that welcome booze-up and crashed out of the crucial freshers socialising period. Thoughts of partying then completely vanished when I realised the weight of my 'ambitious' (completely mental) decision to study Japanese and economics as a dual honours. The first lectures went great, but thereafter- when the *real* work started- I left the hall trembling with panic at my apparent lack of understanding of, well, *anything* related to economics. So, without any friends (because everyone had settled into their groups by now), I spent most of my free time alone in my room, scratching my head at the complex equations in my microeconomics textbook.

I often contemplated what I had got myself into as I heated up my third pot noodle of the day and set the timer on the oven for another processed pie. At first, I romantically conceived the late nights studying alone and frugal lifestyle of spending no more than £15 on weekly food shops as a necessary predecessor to a brighter, more extravagant future. I kept my aspirations on the bigger picture. As the first in my family to attend university, I felt like a trailblazer about to use the platform of higher education as a launchpad to a high-flying career full of money and, err, maybe happiness- I guess? The answer was clear: work now and suffer if you have to- this will all have meaning one day.

Tell me, reader, do you ever struggle to convince yourself that things will be alright when deep down, you know you're chatting bollocks? Looking back, sometimes we're just looking for excuses to justify why we're unhappy. Trying to solve your problems with more work is futile because good grades and a high salary mean nothing when there's nothing else about the world that excites you- work's just a distraction.

It doesn't take long for the 'shut up and work' rhetoric to burn you out; the 'bigger picture' became a blur. The bleak reality stuffed back into the deeper pits of my mind began to break through the cracks. It's the little things I used to notice: groups of friends reuniting after lectures and heading to the pub together, the loud parties in the halls full of cheer and drunken delirium, and the conversations between classmates of which world heritage site they visited at the weekend.

Hang on- they're not really 'little things' are they? They sound like the standard university lifestyle, right? They essentially *are* the typical sights and sounds of the university campus; I only learnt those while they were interrupting my catching up on all the tutorial questions I couldn't do.

Oh, and did I mention that it had only been two weeks? Yeah- I accepted defeat pretty quickly. I was properly on the ropes after only the second round of lectures. The shock horror when I discovered I would have to do this for four years- better get the therapist on speed dial for this chronic imposter syndrome. All sense of time completely disappeared in this otherworldly environment- those two weeks were like a bad fever dream that was all too real.

I remember in my English literature classes at secondary school many of us bonded over our struggles with the challenging work. Hoping to repeat that same bonding experience, I often used the difficulty of economics classes as a conversation starter, only to be met with replies of, 'Actually, I find it really easy.'

'It's not that hard- it's basically common sense.'

'I don't really need the readings, I'm naturally quite good at it.'

… Cheers guys, big help that.

I suppose with some people, if they naturally click with maths then fair enough. But for a considerable number of people who were in the same boat as me, their responses were teeming with arrogance. I'll be honest, a fair bunch of the people I spoke to came across as complete tossers. But hey, as my A-level sociology teacher used to say, you meet people from all walks of life at university.

It's frustrating when you're seemingly the only one sucking at life though, isn't it? Negativity manifested within me for months; soon, even the littlest of things irritated me. Take a set of doors to enter a building: one door is shut and the other is open, traffic is approaching from both sides. Why do people wait in a queue behind the closed door for traffic to pass from the other side, when they could just easily open the door and allow both sets of traffic to pass? Then there were my flatmates who kept leaving cupboard doors open, the kitchen generally being abused, and don't get me started on the bastard who ate all my Cornettoes one evening.

Soon, anyone within a 5-mile radius drove me up the wall one way or another. I felt critical of my lecturers, who were essentially only reading off their PowerPoint slides. I felt critical of university as a whole for being so damn expensive. I felt critical of London for being a dirty and unpleasant city, and for also being bloody expensive. And on top of all that, I felt critical of myself, for being a right miserable git and a fraud- having been so happy, so proud, and so motivated after being accepted into university, I felt ashamed to say I was still the same person now.

To sum up then, here's a nice list of my problems:
- Lack of purpose: *Why am I working this hard? What's it all for?*
- Anxiety: Social situations with so many new people were terrifying. I wouldn't even dare step into my kitchen if I could hear people in there.
- Self-esteem: Every social failure felt like my fault. I believed I was a moody and depressing person who didn't deserve friends.
- Home-sick: No one made me laugh like my old friends could and no overpriced rooftop bar had the same charm as the old club back home.
- Depression: No motivation, no drive. Getting out of bed was a chore and on the weekends I felt content just lying in bed and letting time pass away.

If you are familiar with even just one of these problems then read on, because running helped combat every single one of them. If you aren't familiar with anything on the list then read on anyway, because at some point in your life you will probably have to deal with at least one of them, and with a mindset spurred on by willpower you will know how to run through your problems rather than away from them.

For anyone who has ever experienced a mental health issue, this book is for you. No matter your age, gender, economic situation, anything- we all go through it sometimes in life. I want you to know that running is a free and ever-present tool that will be there for you when all else is lost. Through this sport we return to simpler times. We are kids again, adventuring through the infinite open world. We can move a step back and take a run up into whatever daunting prospects lie ahead. Through running, the ordinary can accomplish the extraordinary. Hopefully this book encourages you to take those first steps.

You always have a choice

I was no fun to be around at the end of 2016. I sat in my classes with a face like a slapped arse and looked very unapproachable. You see, when you look around and see so many happy faces, blissfully enjoying a situation that you feel miserable in, you can't help but despise yourself for being the odd one out.

Why don't I enjoy my studies? Why do I find the work so hard? Why do I dread each class?

… It's because I'm just not good enough, surely.

And with that, a negative spiral resulting in increasing isolation began. So much for uni being the best years of a young person's life.

Okay- so things weren't looking great, but the important thing is that we don't accept dissatisfaction as our norm. I could moan about how tough classes were and how soul draining university was to whoever I wanted- the reality is 80% of people don't care about your problems and the other 20% are glad you have them. At the end of the day it was my problem which I had to solve myself.

Luckily, this is where running then came in. The game changer. Running realigns your focus with what matters. When running, you're in control of your mind and body and nothing else comes in between. When you find harmony within yourself, you lose interest in comparing yourself to others. You can't control what people around you are doing and running helps you realise that by helping you focus on the only person that matters- yourself.

Running put me back in control of the volatility and chaos of my own mind. It reminded me that I am the sole owner of not just my failures, but my successes too. In other words, I make the decisions, because there is always a choice.

Being the sole owner of a problem gives you even greater choice, and for me it was clear: I could passively let my life collapse into self-inflicted isolation and pity, or I could do something radical to try and change it.

By the end of the first term, I realised university wasn't for everyone. Already some of my flatmates and many people in my course had dropped out from the stress of the workload. It was clear that a lot of people also struggled, yet I initially never noticed, because they- like me- hid away in the shadows while the shining smiles of the majority illuminated the whole campus.

When the going got tough, they made a choice, but unfortunately it was the one which set their doubts and fears in stone. By dropping out, they gave themselves zero chance of ever improving their situation. They gave up, and because of that the slightest and most curious chance that their situation could turn favourable was extinguished.

Life is a lot like the stock market: it goes up, it goes down, it has its crashes, but if you stay in the game long enough then you're generally heading on the up. Fleeing upon the first sight of a downturn just because you've taken one L is the *only* way you can ever lose out.

So, it starts with a choice. Do you want to win your internal battles that hold you back in life? Start by choosing to not lose. Start by promising yourself you will never take the option of giving up, because as long as you're still in the running, you're learning and gaining ground every step of the way. Think of winning as simply a case of not losing.

After this promise, I decided there would be no toe-dipping in this venture for betterment. Change had to start with myself. For my first leap forward, I chose to tackle the greatest of all my personal weaknesses: running.

And so, now that we have chosen to change, the next chapter discusses how to prepare ourselves for success, how to discover inspiration and why our reasons are so important. We then join 19-year-old Ellis on a dark winter's evening in the middle of the Kent countryside, where an unforgettable journey of self-discovery and self-empowerment began.

The day you decide to become a runner isn't the day your life changes, it's the day you change your life.

Chapter 2
Finding your inspirations

There's a reason why many of us never complete our goals. It's the same reason we waste money on gym memberships: overreliance on motivation. Without solid inspirations or reasons for taking action, we are left with just motivation. In the short term it's great to feel motivated, but it's unlikely that motivation will consistently stick with us in the long-term. There's no escaping the fact that with every long-term commitment there will be times when our motivation dwindles, or even leaves us completely. Our hard-worked progress may plateau, and we lose that enthusiasm which encouraged us to begin in the first place.

For many people, this occurs in the gym. Many of us make the bold but vague New Year's resolution to 'get fit' and join a gym. Thereafter, the first month is completely game-changing; right in front of your eyes your body is becoming stronger and leaner, and mentally you feel great. You're on top of the world and no one can stop you- you wonder why you never joined the gym sooner and suddenly you feel like you have your entire life on track (whatever 'on track' even means).

Then, after roughly the first month, that motivation gradually fades. The gym starts to feel like a chore, your muscles are not growing as fast and your weight loss is slowing down. The benefits are quickly drying up and you lose motivation. For many people, their will to persist is often tied to their motivation. For that reason, once they lose the will to work out, they quit altogether.

Running has the *potential* to be the same. In fact, any big change you make in your life for the sake of self-improvement can and most likely will suffer the same fate once the novelty wears off. It doesn't have to be like that, and running has far too many benefits and positive spill-overs to give up on. With any long-term commitment, keeping in mind your reasons for taking and continuing action is important for ensuring you don't lose to the inevitable plateau and is the foundation for creating willpower. Setting practical goals in both the long-term and short-term will ensure that the 'long-term' doesn't feel like an endless struggle.

Framing our thoughts

No matter what position of negativity you start from, it is essential to frame your reasons out of positive thoughts in hope for a positive outcome. Choosing a positive change for reasons born out of negative thinking will likely not yield positive results. In doing so, we can lead ourselves down the precisely wrong path of thinking, especially when you word your reasons with strong imperative nuances such as, 'I *need* to get fit', or, 'I *should* be leaner'. These thought patterns cultivate guilt. Starting running because you 'have to', 'must do', or 'should do' would be a shame, because you're subconsciously portraying running as a chore or an errand. At that point, your lifestyle choice is no longer a 'choice', but an obligation.

If you set a goal, by all means hold yourself accountable and if you're really serious, create an obligation to complete it. But refrain from feeling obliged to have goals; if you set a goal without the fundamental aspect of discovering a new avenue for enjoyment or self-fulfilment, then the process will be one largely consisting of misery. Perhaps you do start running and become fitter or lose weight to a certain point, but then you stop when you feel it's no longer required, or when the motivation runs out. The chances are that later down the line you may pile that weight back on, lose all your fitness gains, and have to resort to running again to make things right once more. As you can probably guess, this is a negative cycle a lot of people trap themselves in.

It really shouldn't be that way. No one should start running out of guilt. Even if you weigh 500 stone and are absolutely humungous, or even if you can't walk to the toilet without quadrupling your BPM, running should not just be a mere antidote to your problems. No, running can be so much more than that. It can be something you can enjoy and look forward to, something you can always rely on to pick up your mood, and something that will consistently power you to live a healthier and happier life. If we ever needed a reason to start running, then we can phrase it as simply the desire to live better. It's not just a short-term, nor mid-term pursuit, but rather something that you carry with you through every stage of your life. It shall be the teacher of who you really are in both a physical and mental sense. Whatever changes, whatever turmoil, running is always there for you.

Excuses, ego, and laziness (EEL): The triad of failure

Negative thinking facilitates the impact of excuses, ego, and laziness, or EEL as I like to put it. Excuses are the purest form of laziness, and more often than not, they are the reason we fail to see through our commitments. Be aware that excuses can also be related to ego, which is part of a larger issue. You'll hear absolute rubbish from anyone with an ego. We all know someone who'll rave on about themselves with every opportunity they get. With running- and fitness in general- egos are rife. The worst candidate I often hear is,

'I would start running and do a marathon if I had the time.'

Yeah, and if my uncle had tits he'd be my aunt. Not just for running, but for the sake of anything we ever pursue in our lives, we need to swiftly sweep aside the hypotheticals. I'm sure we know many people who have said something like the above. When I talk to people about running, I hear the marathon statement all too often, and unsurprisingly it's always from non-runners.

Living your entire life with 'I would've ... but I ...' statements is one of the sure signs of an ego problem. You might as well say, 'I would've travelled the globe, solved world poverty, and become a Nobel Peace Prize winner, but my ego was so heavy I couldn't get out of bed. I would've definitely done it, though. Probably.'

Now, I'm not talking about legitimate reasons why we cannot begin certain pursuits, whether they be physical or financial. I'm talking about pure excuses, ego, and laziness- pure EELs. People with an ego problem live their lives convincing themselves they could do something better than others without ever actually doing it. In the context of running, they believe they're a better runner than you without even taking a single step. Ignore those people.

Have you ever struggled with EEL in your life? If you suspect you may have a slight problem with making excuses, or have had in the past, then please don't feel offended, and please don't burn this book in disgust. It's completely normal for us as humans to rationalise a lack of willpower and I've been in this very position countless times in the past, and probably will again in the future as well. Excuses are constantly lurking somewhere in our lives whether intrinsic or extrinsic, and there is little we can do about that. But let's be real with ourselves; please do not neglect the fact that there is a genuine possibility that up until this point in your life you may have held yourself back through either laziness, making excuses, or your ego.

Willpower: The true driver of success

I want to first emphasise that whether you choose running- or any other activity for that matter- willpower will play a huge role in guiding you to success. The Cambridge English Dictionary defines willpower as: 'The ability to control your own thoughts and the way in which you behave.' Meanwhile, Lexico.com defines it as: 'Control exerted to do something or restrain impulses.' Note the phrase 'restrain impulses', this is what we must first fight against. The first step in making a positive change is to identify the impulses, excuses, signs of laziness, or ego problems- whatever you call them- and realise that they may not disappear, but you can still shrug them off.

Notice that in no definition of willpower is the word 'motivation'. This is crucial to note. Motivation comes and goes; it'll be with us at the start when everything is rosy and exciting, but then it'll bog off somewhere else when things get tough. Relying on motivation alone to achieve is very much like sitting alone in a canoe and hoping the wind will eventually blow you to shore. There's a slim possibility of success, but chances are you'll be blown left, right, and centre, and then the wind will die down and you'll be stranded in the middle of a river. What if you just rowed to shore? Yes, it would be tiring, and you'd have to put in a bit of effort. You may even have to row against the wind, but you'll get there. You'll reach the end goal. That's willpower.

Think of willpower as like a muscle, i.e. something that can be trained and become stronger, but also become weaker if you fall into bad habits. So where does running fit into all of this? Well, this is the first positive spill-over effect of our sport. Running helps you build willpower by reinforcing your ability to persevere through times of discomfort and stress. Stronger willpower helped me to continue powering through each page of my university textbooks, even when it all seemed too difficult to ever understand; it kept me on the path that led to the top grades I once considered unreachable.

Willpower is what you need to succeed in the end, not motivation. It's a lovely bonus to be motivated because after all, it's giddiness, it's energy, it's *yeah! I can do this!* But it's unreliable.

Have you ever gone to bed feeling ready to kick arse the next day, only to feel low and full of dread in the morning? Motivation comes and goes and therefore cannot be trusted to consistently support us through our long-term goals. So, stop waiting for the day you'll feel motivated enough, because it will probably never come. Our motivation is not infinite and cannot be trusted to last.

Why have I included this philosophical rambling? Because I feel that nowadays many people are not just turning to running for its physical benefits. Nowadays running is recognised for the mental edge it offers, and many turn to the sport as a means to challenge and develop themselves, which is great, what a bloody good decision you're making. But, to make that a successful decision we have to transition away from our dependence on motivation as soon as possible. The sooner our willpower becomes the driving force in our lives, the sooner we unlock our potential to achieve *absolutely anything*.

Which is why I advocate having clear reasons for when you start running. Having good reasons is what creates and sustains willpower. When you're out alone on the open road with seemingly a million miles to go and the impulses to give up, go home, and forget all about it start to creep in, that's when you can tap into your reasons. If you believe strongly in the reasons why you started, then they will help you continue when things inevitably get tough.

You needn't stress too heavily on having good reasons, instead they can be inspired by what is personal, and maybe even private to you. It's not like you must announce to the entire world your reasons and justifications when you start running, is it? Maybe I am just a private person, but it's no one else's business why you start running. I had many reasons why I began, but everyone only knows one. Mind you, it definitely sounded the best compared to some of the others. I won't hide them from you here- some of my reasons for starting running were rather unusual.

Surrounded by Inspirations

In December 2016, I knew I needed to adapt to all the sudden upheaval life kept throwing. Returning home to Medway and clubbing with my friends again was wonderful nostalgic escapism, but just like the spirits and K cider, its effect eventually wore off. The situation still hadn't changed.

I honestly did not know what to do for a while. The problem I faced being back home was reverting to my old ways in my old life- there was nothing new in sight to possibly propel a struggling boy forward. Or was there?

There's inspiration all around us, in fact. Sometimes you just have to peer deeper into the lives and experiences of those around you. By utilising a bit of empathy, you can imagine yourself in the shoes of someone accomplishing something great or surviving a real pinch situation with a happy ending and it can be incredibly uplifting, particularly when you're down. What about that amazing feeling you get when walking out of the cinema after a great film? It makes *you* want to go out and do something heroic.

Even for my sociopath friends with no capacity for empathy at all, the exercise is as simple as looking at someone doing something great, feeling empowered about it, and thinking, 'Yeah,

I want to feel that way too.' I suppose you could also consider this to be 'positive envy'- hey, whatever gets you inspired. If you're someone who easily feels envious, then use it as a superpower. Use those who impress you as a benchmark, not necessarily for what you want to achieve (envying over Usain Bolt's 100m record won't do you any good), but for how you want to feel.

There is also an element of throwing away your ego here; the egotistical fellow would lament how they could achieve x if they only had y, or if z never occurred. Rather, the humble equivalent would acknowledge the hard work and dedication required to achieve, and realise that is what they currently lack, but can 100% work on. Whoever inspires you is likely on a similar journey, just a few steps further up the road.

When witnessing something great, I try to focus on the positive extrinsic influences, rather than the negative intrinsic influences. This is as simple as changing your mindset from 'Wow that person is so talented, I could never run a marathon because I'm too unfit', to 'Wow that person is so dedicated, they trained hard and finished their first marathon- maybe I could do the same!' See the switch in perspective?

One example of someone who inspires me is the boxing heavyweight champion of the world Tyson Fury. Anyone who knows his story will admire the courage and mental fortitude required to overcome depression and return to the top spot of his profession. However, what I admire about him most is his dogged determination and winning mentality. In his second fight with Deontay Wilder, you can see the fierce look on his face throughout the bout, and it's clear he's in flow state. Every fibre of his being is focussed on the result, on winning, on becoming champion. Every moment of training has gone into producing his most polished performance possible, and what a dominant performance it was. Wilder couldn't touch him. It was beautiful, sheer dominance from start to finish. It is that level of ruthless grit I aspire to emulate. Obviously, it's not realistic for us to become undisputed heavyweight champion of the world, but the mentality to attain that crown is applicable to every goal in our lives.

My influences

I will now tell you about the three main influences that encouraged me to start running. The first one is the rock in my life, the woman who unleashed me into this world 23 years ago and since then has been with me through thick and thin. She's the unbreakable woman with a killer sense of humour and top-class banter. She's none other than my very own mum.

Prior to my decision to start running, Mum had already been a runner herself for almost 10 years. She started in order to get in shape and feel her best self again and has never looked back since. The cool thing about my mum is that she doesn't need to follow trends, nor show off the fact she regularly exercises to the world for a quick ego boost. Nah, she simply does what she wants and thus succeeds at whatever she wants.

When I was around 14, I joined my mum for a run and followed her on my bike. It was an insightful experience to say the least. Mum was in her element, effortlessly gliding across the earth in a smooth and coordinated motion without ever stopping.

Meanwhile, I would labour my throbbing thighs to heave each heavy pedal, where my heart would thumb against my chest and ricochet around my entire torso as I huffed and puffed myself into a nauseous misery- that was just getting to the end of the road.

I spent most of that joint venture outside moaning that I had no stamina. It got to the point where my mum pulled her phone out and started filming me, much like a delinquent teenager would before happy-slapping a nerd, 'Here we see a happy Ellis, battling on, just about to complete his first mile', she commentated. I could only respond with a heavy groan- I hated every moment of it.

Running forms a core part of Mum's daily routine and it ensures she's firing on all cylinders with her work. Fitness-wise, she's ahead of the game compared to most others of the same age. This was also inspiring. If I followed, then perhaps I could beat the inevitable aging process and maybe, just maybe, drastically boost my chances of one day becoming the world's hottest sugar daddy.

Once again, my mum does not feel the need to follow trends or take on big events like marathons. She gets the most out of running and benefits best by simply going out for a few miles three or four times a week. For that reason, she is as successful as any other runner or athlete out there. At the end of the day, she's achieving her goal and feeling much better for it- that's what running's all about.

The second influence is awkward to explain and definitely never mentioned on first dates.

At university, there were two things that got me out of bed each day: 1) the thought of preparing for a new Pokémon VGC tournament, and 2) the excitement of escaping into the world of the Morning Musume, a famous Japanese girl group in the 1990s who were basically Japan's answer to the Spice Girls. In my first year of university I was completely hooked on their music and particularly their famously hilarious television appearances.

When I get hooked on something, it's not long before I find myself scouring the entire internet to discover new knowledge to the point where I become a walking encyclopaedia. With Morning Musume, I would listen to their songs on my way to and from the campus, stay up until 3am every night laughing away at any rare clips of their television appearances I could find on YouTube, and read about all the members' small bits of trivia on fan pages. Back in those days I did have friends, they were just virtual big sisters from 20 years ago.

The connection with running stems from a film called *Pinch Runner*. First things first: this is not a film that is going to wow you with cinematic brilliance. The acting will not enthral you, nor will it probably radiate any kind of artistic value- unless you're like me, I cried towards the end of it. Pinch Runner was a low-budget Japanese film released in May 2000 about a group of high school girls who join their school's running club. They become friends and together they train for an *ekiden* (a type of long-distance running multistage relay race) of half marathon distance as a means to overcome personal challenges in their lives.

The film, alongside its making-of documentaries chronicled not just the trials and tribulations of the film's characters, but the real-life Morning Musume members playing those characters as well. The film spoke to me with a strangely profound impact. As the team reaches the final finish line, the members emotionally reflect on how their experiences together helped them develop as people and build self-belief. The accomplishment of their challenge and climax of the journey was heart-warming, and back in December 2016 that kind of happy ending, in which the process and the result had such a moving and positive impact on the characters, resonated with me *hard*.

Another odd habit of mine- any films or television shows I like, I'll watch again and again[1]. Every time I watch Pinch Runner, I feel inspired and remember that same feeling from the very first time I saw it. It reminds me of the reasons I run and reinvigorates me with excitement to get out there and continue kicking arse.

The feeling I get from Pinch Runner is a feeling you may well receive from any other film about running. When I saw the characters giving their all and growing into greater people, I felt a ping in my stomach that screamed, 'I want to push myself and grow like that. Even if the challenge is steep for me, I want to overcome it. I want to run too.'

It's an unusual source of inspiration, but it struck a chord with me that has remained ever since. Fortunately, you don't have to

---

[1] This is apparently a feature of anxiety, where you derive pleasure and comfort from re-watching television programmes and films because you're assured of how they will end.

commit yourself to very specific interests to get inspired. You just have to empathise. I cared about those characters because they were played by the Morning Musume members that were playing a healing role in my life. As such, it wasn't hard to share their jubilation when they completed the relay race. It was so impactful that I wanted to replicate it myself. Look for people in your life that impress and inspire you; never forget that they started from your position- they started from a choice.

Battling demons

Up until now I've only mentioned external influences- the sole internal influence was what really sealed the deal. That influence came from my past and its numerous failed passions- all of them failures for the same reason: I gave up.

We all dream when we're kids. When I was younger, I wanted to be a footballer, then an actor, then a Formula 1 driver, then a footballer again, and so on. I wanted to stand on the world stage doing something I loved. None of those reached fruition because I always talked myself out of them and threw in the towel.

Out of all these failed careers, my failure as a footballer became one of my main driving forces. Football and I were never a good match. I loved the game, and still do despite having to suffer through watching West Ham every week. I was too shy to join a Sunday league team until I was 15, albeit with a side who were hopelessly rock bottom of their league.

As a teenager, my fitness was catastrophically awful. The managers were always supportive of me, saying the fitness would eventually come, but it never did. In every single match and training session I would almost instantly run out of breath. I couldn't keep up with the pace of the game without my throat giving up. To this day, one of my most humiliating experiences in life is when I ran out of breath just five minutes into a Sunday league match and had to be substituted. My teammates dropped their heads in embarrassment whilst one of the opposition called out, 'Already?!' This haunted me for years.

Soon enough, the thought at the back of my mind that I was chasing an impossible ambition increasingly punctured my confidence. I never made friends with my teammates at the club and we got relegated in my first and only season. I never managed to score or even make an assist whilst I was there; I just never had any confidence in myself. On a couple of occasions after training I would walk back to my mum's car holding back tears, because deep down I knew I was never good enough. I wasn't talented enough, and I was wasting my time believing in a dream that would never come true.

In hindsight, my attitude was the first barrier to success. I never worked hard enough to earn any achievements. I just never strove to improve myself, and that I used to really regret. Back then, I didn't believe that with hard work and consistency over a long period of time I could become a better player. I never had the long-term vision to realise that. Instead, I wanted all the skills and fitness at once without having to work for it. For that, I failed. And I'm glad I did, in a strange way, because eventually it led me to the day when I decided to grow up and learn how to earn success.

And so, on 27th December 2016 I made a big decision. It was right at the beginning of that hazy period in which Christmas Day and Boxing Day are both over, and you just cannot figure out what day it is before New Year's as you blissfully live off selection boxes and turkey sandwiches.

Usually, I would be relaxed during a time of no worries nor responsibilities, but this time I became buoyant with ambition. I was ready to change. I was ready to become better. I took in the inspiration from my mum, I took in the inspiration from Pinch Runner, and I took in the inspiration from past failures as the catalyst in changing my mindset. I decided to pour faith in the examples shown by Mum and Morning Musume, the examples demonstrating that if you dedicate yourself and work hard enough at something in the long term, then you can achieve great things you once never thought possible.

Running may have always been my weak point, and I knew that I might not ever become brilliant at it. But that wasn't the point, the point was to overcome my weakness. I wanted to work hard and prove to myself that if I can triumph over my weakness of running with hard work, then I can achieve the very same with my economics classes at university. This was about proving that weaknesses are not set in stone.

That cold day in December was the day a fire lit inside my belly, and that wasn't because I ate the Christmas pudding with the flame still roaring on top. It was the day I pledged to become a runner. My goal? To run a full-length, 26.2-mile marathon.

At first glance, marathon training plans took approximately four months, so I searched for events in May to give myself plenty of time. No rush. I discovered the perfect event- the Kent Circuit Marathon. It would take place just down the road from where my nan lives, 5 months in the future, on 27th May 2017. It would be the perfect chance to show my efforts to Mum and Nan.

I sat glued to my laptop screen and pondered the event for a while. *Do I really want to do this?* Everything looked to be in place, everything looked so exciting. I considered letting the thought marinate, but then opted to throw all caution to the wind. Sometimes you just have to click the damn button, because there was absolutely no excuse *not* to enter. The more I thought about it the higher the likelihood I would start rationalising reasons not to enter. No- this time no EELs would block my escape from the rut. I switched my overactive brain off, silenced all the doubting voices, and signed up for my first ever marathon. It was official then: I would be running a marathon in May next year.

As soon as the confirmation email landed in my inbox I was overcome by the purest surge of excitement, the sort that I hadn't felt since before university started. That excitement wasn't all for the desired end goal, but for the journey. I wanted to see just how difficult it could get and how I, a failure up to this point, would react to hardships.

Mum was sat nearby leisurely enjoying a cup of tea when I told her that I had signed up to a marathon. Safe to say she was delighted. She stood up and gave me a big hug and seemed so pleased. She said she was proud of me for taking on such a challenge, and that in itself felt like one huge achievement already.

Chapter 3
Your first run is no one else's business

As the tedious cliché goes: New Year, New Me. In the days leading up to New Year's, I harvested inspiration. I watched the stories of people accomplishing their first marathon, the dramatic transformations of those who went from rock bottom to discovering their best self through running, and I watched Pinch Runner, over and over again.

I was so ready to begin. I said goodbye to 2016 in suitable style, by getting rather annihilated on K cider with some of my best mates, Ethan, Gianni, Mark, and Joe. We belted out Auld Lang Syne, danced around the room to our favourite tunes, and then eventually conked out and crashed on the sofas.

I woke up to the sound of my mates' drunken snoring, splitting the silence of the new year's first dawning. Luckily, I never seem to get hangovers the following day after drinking (to which some might say, 'you ain't going hard enough Ellis!'), and so I felt ready to get out there and get cracking- *this is it.*

I looked into Mark's bathroom mirror and felt like an improved man already, even upon noticing that I had chipped a tooth last night from gripping a beer can in my mouth. Alongside that, for breakfast my mates and I made what were probably the greasiest pancakes possible, bathing them in maple syrup, but of course lining them with a few berries on top for the health benefits. By 11am we were ready to depart Mark's gaff and I dropped the others back at their homes.

Once I saw off Ethan, I paused in my car alone. *This was it.* True adrenaline hit me. It was now just me, my Peugeot 206, and the open road for the first time in this new era. I may have been simply driving home, but at the same time I felt as if I were driving towards a greater future. To be more specific, I was driving towards my first ever run.

The beauty of simplicity

The aim right from the outset with my early runs was to keep things simple. I reset everything I knew about myself and running to the very basics. I envisioned starting from zero, and building a stronger, better version of myself from the ground up. This kind of approach is easy to take with running because the sport is so wonderfully straightforward. Running is one of those great endeavours that is easy to learn but has infinite challenges and feats to accomplish. There's a plethora of personal trials waiting for you, if you so choose. Anyone can run, but to achieve true personal greatness- however you may define it- requires hard work, dedication, and a growth mindset over the long term. Each and every one of us is capable of all three.

The single greatest advantage this approach offered was the reassurance that absolutely nothing could go wrong. I knew I had it all to gain and nothing to lose as I sang away to Morning Musume in excitement and optimism for the future ahead. It wouldn't matter if I threw up with each step or ran out of breath after five minutes- as long as I didn't break any bones then simply going out for my run and coming back in itself would be an accomplishment. After all, even if I only managed a mile, it would still be one mile more than most of the hungover population on New Year's Day.

Good habits and productivity start from simple things. A simplified, nothing-to-lose strategy for running will guide you into gradually attempting tougher challenges, perhaps even leading all the way up to a marathon. We can apply this approach to our everyday lives as well. Ultra-marathoner and mental health campaigner Ben Robertson once said that the simple task of making your bed after you wake up will positively impact your productivity for the rest of the day. By doing so, you already complete one task which rewards you with a sense of accomplishment, encouraging you to go and tackle the rest of your tasks.

Another advantage of going back to basics is alleviating any pressure to make a return on your investment of time and money. Avoid forcing yourself into any commitments early on; some may decide they're going to become a runner and invest in expensive clothing and extortionate gadgets to get them started, but then at that point they're too financially invested to turn back. By the slim chance running just doesn't work out for you, you'll find yourself with a thinner wallet and lots of unused equipment. Mind you, this is worse with other sports- my rusty bike tells a sorry tale.

The beauty of running is that you can enjoy every benefit without having to spend a penny- much like how video games used to be before DLC. Of course, you can buy all the branded clothes and equipment, but when you think about it, any purchase you make is optional. In fact, you don't even need shoes to run- according to the *Born to Run* school of thought, running in bare foot or 'minimalist' shoes with thin soles replicates the natural action humans perform when running and may be preferable to running with heavily cushioned shoes. Shoes or no shoes, cushioned or thin soles, you can try them all. We're all different.

I unknowingly started off minimalist with my football trainers and found no issues early on. Mind you, there is a reason most running shoes have cushioned heels and that's because it absorbs the shock from your feet pounding against the ground, preventing injuries. Over time that stress on your joints and bones can accumulate, and if you're not careful, could result in a nasty stress fracture. If you ever visit a running shop, give all the different models a try with their in-store treadmill. If you want to see which running shoes are most popular at the moment, then RunRepeat.com provides rankings along with a round-up of reviews to help you pick the right pair.

Even though I began my first couple of runs in football trainers, I soon ordered my first ever pair of running shoes online. I picked up the most basic model from a trusted brand- a £30 pair of New Balance running shoes in a lovely royal blue (matched my car). Starting out cheap is advisable, because most top of the range running shoes are priced well into triple figures. You can pay extra for all the overhyped cushioning technology, but when you're first starting out it's wise to get a basic pair that will do the job. The good thing is most of the leading brands also create cheaper versions of their mainline products which are sold at high street retailers; my shoes were ordered from Next- hardly a recognised running brand! The quality can of course vary, but if you buy from a good brand you should expect solid durability- my first New Balance shoes managed well over 1,000 miles.

When it came to running clothes, I used any sports T-shirt and shorts I could find in the deepest depths of my wardrobe. Again, more expensive options are available from big brands, but just remember that for the time being at least, they are nothing more than options. Running is one of the rare activities that can be done with attire that you probably already have- let's milk the most of this cow by starting off our running careers for free. Further down the line we can embrace the technical prowess of the top brands by purchasing special sweat-wicking shirts, socks with more technology in their fabrics than the rocket that first took man to the moon, and my personal favourite- running pants with inbuilt bollock support. It's all there waiting for you, but first let's enjoy the simplicity of the most accessible sport on the planet.

Goals: Why you might want to keep your mouth shut

Keeping things low-key was another big part of my approach to running. The temptation to announce to the world that I was taking my first steps ahead of a bold new journey was there, but instead I made sure this first run was my business only- probably for the best as I couldn't expect too great a performance with multiple litres of alcohol slushing around in my stomach. No, my plans and ambitions were strictly private for the time being, which leads us to an important point.

Setting goals is great. We all know that, but announcing them? There are two ways about it. On the one hand, if you stand up and proclaim to the world your big life-changing plans, there are decent chances that many in your close circles will support you. Friends and family always want to see you happy and successful- well, most of the time. Your extended network may or may not be as supportive. Work colleagues, classmates, etc., you can get some right killjoys poisoned with envy who would love to see you fail. After all, it's the only thing that makes those people feel better.

With running, you are embarking on a long-term journey that will take you miles beyond the self-pitying non-action-takers of life. It sounds great but bear in mind that there is always the possibility that a few people won't want you to accomplish any kind of greatness. Naysayers, killjoys, party-poopers- whatever you call them- they exist. You may be unfortunate enough to know some of these types of people in your life already, but in case you need a hint on how to spot them, just listen out for the classic,

'But running is bad for your knees!'

Promise me that as soon as you hear that statement, you'll switch your brain off and save your ears for something worth hearing. We'll deal with The Great Knee Debate properly in chapter 7 and put the issue to bed once and for all.

With regards to those negative people in your life, realise that by announcing your goals to them they will silently wait in the shadows for that mute satisfaction of watching you fail. Now realise that by keeping your goals private until they reach fruition, you'll eventually be able to speak openly of your achievements while the naysayers receive double the irritation from not just your accomplishment, but seeing you announce it out of the blue and make it look so simple and easy. I'm getting a little side-tracked here- for those with a competitive flare in their lives it may make for good sport but remember first and foremost that you should never value your personal achievements in comparison to others- the only comparison is between the person you used to be and the person you are now.

Keeping your goals and ambitions private until they reach maturity is usually a smart strategy. Why? Because it takes a lot of the pressure off you. It allows you more time to concentrate solely on yourself and if things go wrong- which they inevitably will at some point- you can actually enjoy your failures and spend as much time as you need learning from them.

While I set myself the goal of running a marathon in May, I believed I wouldn't be too heartbroken if I failed to complete the 26.2 miles. It would of course be a failure, but under the scrutiny of my surrounding circles and the external pressure from people doubting my abilities to plan, train, and run, the potential marathon mishap would become a rather miserable experience. Because the goal was private, I viewed the potential for failure as another exciting chapter in my personal story. I know myself best, and I knew that if I fail then it'll only add to the drama, the emotion, and the sense of accomplishment I feel on the grand day I do cross the finish line after 26.2 miles, whenever that may be. Others might not see it that way, therefore you needn't include them in your plans.

Interestingly, there are numerous studies to suggest that those who announce their goals prematurely or on impulse are more likely to fail in their endeavours.[2] The reason for this is that by announcing your goals, your brain believes you have already accomplished something, creating a false sense of effort that lowers our drive to put in the *actual* work. This is known as 'action faking', whereby you take action or partake in an activity that lures you into a sense of making steps towards your goal, when in actual fact the action had no real impact on your progress at all.

At the end of the day, it is easier to just keep your gob shut and let your results do the talking. With big changes, we don't need people's eyes staring at our every movement. We don't need others' judgements. The activity of running doesn't require any other individual to partake- it is the purest form of harmony between the mind and body. The more the two work in tandem,

---

[2] Gollwitzer, P. M., Sheeran, P., Michalski, V., & Seifert, A. E. (2009). When Intentions Go Public: Does Social Reality Widen the Intention-Behavior Gap? Psychological Science, 20(5), 612–618. https://doi.org/10.1111/j.1467-9280.2009.02336.x

the more you learn about yourself. No one else needs to come in between that- running can be as private as you want it to be.

There are of course times when you might like to share your goals. If you're running for charity, then it's in your best interest to keep followers and donors updated on your progress to rally further support. However, you can decide how public you make your campaign, which is something we will talk about further in chapter 8. If you want to welcome people into your relationship with running and go polygamous then that's fine. Personal trainers, coaches, nutrition experts, even a masseuse if you're minted, can add a lot of value to your running goals. But this book is about the simple relationship between running and us as individuals, so we'll keep it that way from now on.

Nurtured by nature

When I finally returned home on New Year's Day, I didn't bother showering before my run and instead got changed straight into my sports gear. I wolfed down a bowl of granola and waited impatiently for my stomach to digest every last oat. Five minutes passed and little progress was made, prompting me to start lacing up my trainers with a litre of milk sitting on top of last night's beer. I felt ready enough to go. I approached the back door, where a slight sensation of angst tapped me on the shoulder; for once I was leaving the house with empty hands and empty pockets- no phone, no keys, no wallet.

Boy was I now glad to live in a rural area. When I set foot from the gravel driveway onto the narrow country roads, I was enveloped in a paradise of greenery; trees replaced buildings and animals replaced gangs of students- a step into the *real* world.

Upon taking to the tarmac, I suddenly had a platform to be open and honest with myself in terms of how I felt both physically and mentally. If you ever need to clear some head space, think something through deeply, or just have a pretend argument with yourself, then solitary running is one of the best means to do so.

If you can, I recommend running in the most natural environment possible. I would even go as far to say that it is worth a few train stops, or a thirty-minute drive if it means you can access a less crowded, more rural area. At the very least, try to find a nice park nearby. The reasons for this are plentiful, especially for new runners. Firstly, you can better avoid distractions. In cities, these usually arise from the bustling main roads, police sirens, car and pedestrian traffic, and the general sensory overload of bright lights all around you. My room in London was situated in student halls of over 400 occupants; I lived on the ground floor, right next to the entrance. It was also next to a main road, five minutes from King's Cross St Pancras Station. As you can imagine, my ears were assaulted with constant noise both indoors and out. This made switching off as hard as it could be, and every time I returned home to the countryside the difference was stark.

Running in rural locations allows you to disconnect from the world around you and amongst the silent solitude, concentrate on mindfulness- a key element in enjoying a good run. Mindfulness is defined by concentrating focus on your present situation by acknowledging and accepting your thoughts, feelings, and bodily sensations; it is a feature of running as well as meditation. Now, try achieving that when you're waiting nervously at a crossing whilst a taxi driver and moped rider exchange a bit of verbal venom, just as the exhausted sod driving a double-decker bus goes steaming past a set of red lights. It's happened before and I can say from personal experience it's not particularly therapeutic.

Speaking of therapeutic, here's a second point. Running alone with no one nearby allows you to be your true self and vent whatever kinds of thoughts and feelings you wish to unleash. We often go through our daily lives harbouring all kinds of internal lamentations that we know we could never, ever directly express. One of your friends being a tosser? Let mother nature know. Feeling the inclination to tell your boss to go do one? Let mother nature know. Exchanged verbal blows with someone but couldn't conjure up the correct comeback at the most crucial moment? Let mother nature know. I am of course, alluding to the idea that talking to yourself, or even having full-blown arguments, is a strange but surprisingly superb therapeutic technique to unload any of your recent woes. You might feel like a bit of a berk doing it at first- and certainly try to avoid any eye-contact if you have to run in a busy area- but you'll feel damn great afterwards. The stats speak for themselves: I have won 100% of my arguments when out running.

Stepping with stitches

Physically, my first run was much better than I could have imagined. Many of us picture ourselves running and assume a loss of breath by the time we've reached the end of the road. I expected just that, considering my lack of exercise, highly processed diet, and recent drinking antics. But I got a pleasant surprise- let me just remind you that I'm still the same person who ran out of breath after five minutes of their Sunday league matches- even I, with the world's worst stamina and a stomach ready to explode with granola and Stella, managed to complete my planned distance.

At the very beginning, I cherished every step. I lifted off from my heels to initiate the running motion with my head fixated on gazing down at the history-making movements of my feet- I knew this was the start of something great. The opening ten minutes were grand and full of joy. 'I'm doing it!' my mind cheered, just like a kid riding a bike without stabilisers for the first time.

After cautiously exerting slightly more energy through my thighs to negotiate a long winding incline, the top of the hill rewarded me with scenery of the gorgeous and boundless English countryside, followed by a long gradual decline ahead. It's the little rewards that are always the most exciting, and in the beginning, it taught me deferred gratification at its most simple level: if I persist in climbing this hill, then I get to enjoy a nice downhill slope afterwards to relax.

Once the slope levelled out, I switched terrains onto soil and navigated my way through a tight tunnel of bushes before leaping over the gate to a bumpy gravel straight. The adrenaline of rushing through the narrow and muddy trail spurred me to pick up the pace, to which my overexuberance was then punished by a crippling stitch, the equivalent of taking a gunshot to the stomach. The joyride was over at that point, my stomach screamed while my granola and alcohol smoothie had also caught up on me. I feared a gaping hole would open up in my gut and the whole of last night would come pouring out. Nevertheless, I tried to keep moving forward, regardless of whether I was running, walking, or crawling. At times I did walk and at other times I needed to stop completely. No frustration would penetrate my armour of rationality though- the aim was to complete the distance with nothing too fancy on top. I kept my expectations low and as such, I achieved my aim with no qualms nor regrets.

Completing the distance- that's what it's all about! My first 'run', wasn't just a run, but a series of walking breaks, stitch-soothing sessions, and stops to pat my chest in order to release a bellowing beery burp. I ran as much as I could and stopped when I needed. I returned home with two stitches and two rather shell-shocked legs, but also with the knowledge and pride that I had completed 4.5 miles. It doesn't sound like much, but the previous 'me', the 2016-spec Ellis, would have done zero miles. I reached my short-term, daily goal: to complete the distance. With this accomplishment recorded in my journal, I knew I had made my first small step towards the larger endeavour.

Mentally, my first run was spirit-cleansing (and lung-cleansing too, I wish my mates didn't smoke so much). After one term of university where in every class I saw myself as the dumbest person in the room, my self-esteem was rock bottom. So to know that I had accomplished something seemingly small yet part of something so much bigger all on my own accord was massive and it injected me with the belief that even more was possible. The back-to-basics approach worked.

My first 'runner's high'

Once I got home, it was all smiles. I felt *bloody amazing*. It was my first true experience of the 'runner's high', and I became instantly addicted. If ever there was a reason to get out there and start running straight away, then this is it. The runner's high is the term used to describe the blissful feeling of sheer happiness and euphoria following a run. It crushes any feelings of anxiety and makes you buoyant with belief that you can take on absolutely any obstacle thrown your way. Pretty amazing, right? For anyone feeling sceptical, let me get scientific.

The runner's high is caused by endorphins- the happy chemicals produced by your brain that evoke elevated feelings of calmness and brighter moods. Specifically, these endorphins are created in the prefrontal and limbic regions of the brain- the areas associated with emotions related to love. So, if you're familiar with that lovey-dovey warm feeling you get when you fancy the living daylights out of someone, then imagine that, but towards your entire life in general.

Additionally, running at levels which tests your body's capabilities increases the levels of endocannabinoid, which funnily enough is a natural version of the 'buzz' chemical from marijuana, hence the name, 'runner's high'. It's crazy isn't it, one minute you're Sir Mo Farah, the next you're Kurt Cobain. Thanks to the runner's high, I could finally feel at ease when with my 'weed friends'; whenever they light the dank, all I have to do is say 'One sec, my *gnarly dudes*, I'm just gonna go run for a bit', and then we're all high together.

Jokes aside- and I should reiterate that the runner's high and drug-induced 'highs' are completely different- the runner's high is what will drive you to keep striving for more. Imagine feeling addicted to productivity and positivity? I once read a quote in *Runner's World* that said if you could put all the benefits of running into a single pill and sell it, then you would be an instant billionaire. Moreover, to achieve greater runner's highs, you're naturally incentivised to find a level in your run that challenges your physical limits but is not your maximum. Hence, you don't need to go all out in every run to feel good afterwards, in fact doing so might have the opposite effect. Rather, you should aim for 70 to 85 percent of your age-adjusted maximum heart rate. To calculate your maximum heart rate, subtract your age from 220. So, for a 25-year-old, the maximum heart rate would be 195, and the runner's high 'sweet spot' would be approximately between 136 and 166 beats per minute.

But that's being very specific and for the time being we aren't too concerned about fancy measurements. To achieve the runner's high, you simply need to push yourself. If it's uncomfortable and you feel the urge to stop, then you're probably doing it right. If something hurts, or you feel like you're about to vomit all over the beautiful countryside then you need to relax mate. My first runner's high was the ultimate bonus to what was already a monumental moment. 2017 was off to a flyer.

After a few more runs of the same distance, I quickly began to see small improvements. Namely the fact that I wasn't getting such extreme stitches anymore, although I think we all know why that was in the first place (hint: don't go out on a full stomach!). My body also felt more 'ready' for action each time I set out as the muscle memory of my running posture consolidated itself.

I also found my marathon training plan, which we shall see in the next chapter. The start-date for my 17-week life-changing training would be 30th January, allowing time to tune up to an adequate level of fitness before things really kicked off. My new running shoes had also arrived- everything was coming together!

At this stage, the thought of returning to London for another university term no longer haunted me. I saw it as a beatable challenge if taken one step at a time, like my early runs. As we reach the end of this chapter, I want to draw your attention back to the title- your first run really isn't anyone's business. In 2017's infant stages I felt as if I was slowly gaining the ability to yield a great power- the power to significantly enhance my productivity from running. No one needed to know, because already at this stage, they wouldn't get it. I realised that the more I ran and the further I studied the sport, the closer I came to entering the exclusive, illustrious, secret-but-not-so-secret club of runners, i.e. a group of individuals sharing the same passion for a wonderful sport that makes you feel great in the short run, and develops you into a more capable human being in the long run.

The early euphoria of running had gripped me. I wasn't just ready to take on this marathon, but I was ready to take on university and make it a better experience. As the next chapter chronicles, once back in London I had an epiphany. Everything clicked. I went on to have the most productive period of my entire life with running pulling the strings every step of the way.

It's amazing to think how far we've progressed already: it starts with a choice, followed by reasons, and then a simple, nothing-to-lose-all-to-gain approach. Before you know it, and as if by magic, the impossible becomes reality.

Chapter 4
The early euphoria of running

The new term begins. A return to the capital for a second crack at university- this time equipped with the powers of running.

I anticipated the moment I would strut through the reception doors as a changed man. The reception staff would double-take and remark, 'Since when did that diamond don live with us?' just as I return to my room, unleash my belongings, and call the place my home for the first time. I looked forward to meeting my flatmates, especially seeing as since the second day I had withdrawn to my room and lived as a hermit. Perhaps this time the kitchen small talk wouldn't be as awkward! Maybe I might even learn their names.

But then came the wobble. As London skyscrapers appeared on the horizon, *that* familiar dread returned. I remembered I had a lot of work to do. I remembered I was still lagging behind. I remembered the responsibility was all mine. During the journey to the capital, my anxiety gradually rose. The complex of skyscrapers swallowed me up after the Blackwall tunnel, and an overwhelming sense of angst spawned behind my back to shaft me up the rear.

Once again it was just me against the world. The songs of birds amidst the countryside tranquillity were replaced by the usual sirens and motorbikes, until I heard a new type of commotion: a cab driver shouting, 'You've trod shit all over my mats! I'm gonna call the police!' The familiar and beloved faces of the Medway towns were also replaced by unknown, frowning faces on every corner of the street. My approach: hands in pockets, head down, mind my own business- don't want my own resting bitch face to get me into any scuffles now.

Once back at the halls, things weren't going quite as I imagined. Rather than puffing my chest out and emphatically announcing my presence, I clumsily stumbled through the double doors, struggling with my heavy suitcase. Intimidated by the student atmosphere, I then rushed to my room and hastily locked the door. Guaranteed solitude. Everything was how I left it- the shower drain blocked, desk full of crumbs, and that cheap bedding set with a duvet as thin as tissue still unwashed. I knew how lucky I was to have cheap accommodation- or any accommodation at all- in zone 1 of London, but again, the thought that someone deserved to be there more than me intruded my mind.

I began unpacking but didn't finish. Suddenly, I didn't want to unpack. Suddenly, what was initially a simple formality now felt like a massive task. Already the run-away instincts cried to give up and go home. I was awestruck by it all. The weight of every task from turning around my university experience to going out and buying groceries for the coming week- everything seemed too overwhelming. I knew I had to get food, or I would probably go the whole of tomorrow without eating due to the bulk of classes. I knew I had to take action, but I just didn't want to take responsibility for myself. I just wanted to stay there and hide from the world. I sat on my bed for a while and let myself sob into a pillow at the thought of it all- the thought that it was all up to me. At least no one could see me. No one could see me wince from adult responsibility. I didn't want to fight the world, nor did I want to face another term at university. I escaped from reality by playing a slow, comforting song from Morning Musume, and tried to fall asleep.

As you can see, I had an awful mood swing here. Excitement quickly turned to anxiety, and then that anxiety facilitated the depressive episode in the evening. Mental health can be like that. Just a few runs in and I felt like I was ready to conquer the world. But dealing with anxiety isn't a straightforward process. It has elations and deflations- this occasion was definitely the latter.

Although running introduces such an instantaneous boost, it's important to note that its greatest effects are not yielded overnight. In the short term I may have learnt the runner's high, but that wasn't enough to fix the larger, underlying issues with university; it's important to remember that a good mood and a healthy mind are not the same thing. Moreover, volatile moods and pungent bursts of motivation can be detrimental to long term progress if they are not moderated, otherwise they can feed impulsivity. The reason I mention this is because I want you to read this chapter with a critical eye. Am I operating on motivation or willpower? The reason for this is to consolidate the distinction between the two. The story I'm about to tell may resonate with many runners as they probably had a similar experience in their early days. The early euphoria of running yielded extraordinary results over the first fortnight, but I failed to acknowledge the numerous underlying flaws in my approach. See if you can find them.

The parallels of marathons and exams

The first day back was horrific. The same face-like-thunder that stormed the campus had returned- I wanted not a single word with anyone within a hundred metres of me. Throughout my classes I passively participated from the furthest corner on each lecture hall and tried to go the whole day without being seen, which wasn't too hard. When I returned home that rainy afternoon, I kept kicking myself for being an utter failure. From the very outset, I had already thrown all my personal resolutions down the drain. It seemed like I was enrolled for another term of misery.

Once indoors, I wanted no recollection of the day at university. I threw my bag out of sight, booted up my laptop and opened my marathon training schedule. Excitement ensured- something worth looking forward to. It was the 17-week beginner training plan from the London Marathon website[3]- a great plan for any new runners looking to challenge their first marathon. It was still

---

[3] https://www.virginmoneylondonmarathon.com/trainingplans/beginner-17-week-training-plan/

three weeks before the scheduled start date. How I wished it would start sooner. At that point I began to imagine the gradual challenges I would overcome, namely through the increased distance of my long runs. The more I read, the more the buzz returned. I gazed at week 1, the 'easy' beginning of my journey:

Week 1	
Monday	Rest
Tuesday	10-min walk, 20-min ER, 5-min walk
Wednesday	Rest
Thursday	10-min walk, 30-min ER, 5-min walk
Friday	Core & Stretching
Saturday/Sunday	5-min walk, 30-min LR, 5-min walk, 10-min ER, 5-min walk

Let's first start with the acronyms: 'ER' stands for 'easy run', while 'LR' means 'long run'. Simple enough, right? Now, you may look at that table and think, 'Gosh I don't know if I could do a 55-minute outing on the first week', or you might scoff, 'Ha! Looks so easy.' Regardless of your level at the start, the first week gently pushes you to immediately adapt to a new routine of running three days a week and dedicate yourself to at least a day of working on your core muscles and stretching your body.

From my desk I marvelled at its simplicity. The first week would be the steppingstone for much harder sessions to follow and an important test of discipline. Could I commit to the routine? Could I complete each walking and running segment in accordance with the schedule- no more, no less? These little personal challenges were fantastically exciting.

I then scrolled down to week 12, where things would get serious and much more complex:

Week 12	
Monday	Rest
Tuesday	50-min ER
Wednesday	Rest
Thursday	10-min ER, 3x (8-min TR, 2-min ER), 5x 30-sec fast, 5-min ER
Friday	Core & Stretching
Saturday/Sunday	18 miles LR: 3x 4 miles MP at start, middle, and end

Here we have a couple of extra acronyms: 'TR' for 'threshold run', and 'MP' for 'marathon pace'. A threshold run requires you to run faster than your normal 'comfortable' effort (let's say 'comfortable' is where you can just about maintain a conversation), but not at your absolute limit. Your marathon pace is pretty self-explanatory, it is the pace per mile/kilometre required to maintain as an average throughout the marathon to hit your goal time. For example, to run a marathon in under 4-hours, you would need to average 9-minute miles.

I disregarded the marathon pace and replaced it with my own comfortable pace because I did not have a time goal- I just aimed to finish. Viewing week 12 was a humbling experience- I knew that in my current state I was 100% unable to complete it and still feel my pulse at the end- this was hugely exciting. It was a peek into the future where running 18 miles would be achievable.

Looking at the gradual increase in mileage and intensity, every week played an equally important part in preparation for the marathon. To be successful with this schedule required faith. This meant following it one session at a time and completing the requirements without going any further or risk jeopardising the next session. Consistent effort in the short-term would eventually culminate to achieve the long-term objective. In other words, we cannot achieve long-term success instantly (hardly a news flash). Rather, it is by consistently achieving lots of short-term goals that eventually allows us to reach our end goal.

Then came the single biggest breakthrough in my undergraduate career. I realised that marathons are a lot like exams. When it comes to important exams, cramming the night before won't give you excellent results. You may achieve average results, or even 'good' results, but unless you're a lucky sod then cramming is never a smart tactic. Similarly, you cannot run a marathon by cramming in 50 miles the night before. Instead, training for a marathon requires months of consistent work to prepare you for the big event. Likewise, achieving excellent exam results requires months of consistent and comprehensive work to be able to arrive on the big day of the exam and know exactly what to write when you turn over the question paper.

The long-term goal of completing a marathon required multiple short-term efforts, which would be each week of training.

So, if I could plan a strategic roadmap towards success for running, then surely the same was possible with university work? Suddenly, there appeared light at the end of the tunnel for my impossible economics classes. By planning ahead for the end goal and splitting each task required to reach it into the weeks ahead, university magically then seemed doable.

Now the mental cogs were turning. Ideas and inspiration and belief, all steaming out of my ears like a flipping kettle. It had taken a day since I returned to London, but the wait was worth it- Motivation surged.

The epiphany

Seriously, I believed I had just discovered the secret to success not just for a 19-year-old student, but for *life*. It was a game-changing breakthrough. From then on, the anxiety dissipated and the excitement, coupled with ambition, returned. From this very moment I would turn it all around through the power of long-term planning.

I had my marathon plan, now I just needed a study plan- but why stop there? How about a diet plan? A shopping plan? Even a budgeting plan? Ideas sprouted from every crevice of my brain. I then pondered, improvement doesn't just have to cover today and tomorrow; maybe we can save yesterday. What if I went through every week of lecturers and tutorials, produced detailed notes on them and set them aside for future revision? What if I covered a week of work a day for the next two weeks, spread across my four modules? I don't have any assignments until the end of the term, so why don't I make this free time now the most productive it can be? The brainstorm flourished further as I whipped up another Word document to begin chunking the tasks required for Operation: Save Term 1.

I frantically typed away my module topics and ordered them into separate days. The task in hand wouldn't be a lark: one week's work from a single economics module involved multiple readings of long and boring academic texts mixed with impossible mathematics that take at least four hours and one therapy session to comprehend. It would be a big effort, but on paper I could see the bigger picture: by concentrating my efforts on what could be covered in a single day over a ten day period, I would have caught up with an entire term's worth of work in under two weeks- this was the key motivating factor. I knew it would require work, but by equally distributing my energy across a realistic timespan, it seemed absolutely possible. The key takeaway here is the power of chunking, any audacious task can be completed in a timely manner by splitting it into manageable chunks with a clear view of when your end date will be. When I set out to tackle this workload, the thought of being done in only ten days alone motivated me- I just had to put the plan into action.

Unsurprisingly, I didn't sleep well that night; my brain bounced off the walls with ideas on how to chunk my entire life. Once the morning dawned, the most productive fortnight in Ellis history began.

Main task 1: Wake up and run
Morning. 7:30am, explode from the sheets. Breakfast. Weetabix with kiwi on top, plus a coffee. Digest, then stretch to feel awake and ready to exercise. Get out the front door by 9am. Begin running.

My first run in London was very different to my countryside adventures. It was my very first time going out with my new running shoes, which up to that point I had only ever held very carefully in my hands with fascination, like they were fragile artefacts. The mesh toe box, padded heels, and thick cushioned soles appeared otherworldly to me. I felt like I was holding two small blue spaceships. Wearing them was even more peculiar. They're like moon boots; suddenly I'm two inches taller and bouncing all over the gaff. With each step I travelled upwards rather than forwards! At least my feet felt supported.

I swiped my card to exit from the halls' main entrance and felt the icy wind of a brutal January morning sink its claws into my face. Maybe just a T-shirt wasn't the best idea. I walked for five minutes and then broke into running motion. Having already grown accustomed to the gorgeous natural sights of the countryside, running up a London back alley before being stopped by a million traffic lights proved to be a hollow experience.

I ran laps around Russell Square Gardens, which is a bit on the small side for running. With each lap around 0.3 miles, you would have to go around fifteen times to achieve five miles. As to how much you can tolerate that kind of repetition is up to you, but at this early point in my running career I didn't mind. I opted to do

12 laps to complete 4 miles, running in the same anti-clockwise direction each time, passing by the same scenery, over and over. None of that bothered me. I just felt great to be out and exercising. To think I was a runner in London felt very cool.

I timed the early runs on my iPhone stopwatch and made a short note of each session's duration. I aimed to complete 6 miles with every session, three times a week, and note how my pace increased. Every time I would try to push a little bit harder; remain at a comfortable pace up to the fourth mile and then give it full beans on the way back. The results were hugely promising. I gained minutes over the course of a few days and each time the runner's high left me feeling euphoric and accomplished at the end. That post-run buzz always spurred me onto my next task.

A few notes on running in the city

If you live in the city, it's more than worth running whatever distance necessary, or even taking public transport, in order to reach a public park. Running along the pavements will infuriate you as much as it disrupts your rhythm from constantly having to stop. The worst example is without a doubt any street near King's Cross; you find yourself constantly weaving in and out of pedestrians and accidentally bulldozing those that randomly stop in the middle of the street. Failure to be vigilant can also make you look like a right muppet, like the time I once ran straight into a lamppost for peering too far into the distance, completely missing the giant metal pole in front of me.

For Londoners, there are plenty of good running spots to choose from. Regent's Park is a personal favourite; it has many routes, much to see, and is usually not too crowded. I also once saw Dermot O'Leary, and ran past Jimmy Carr, so if you're into celeb-watching then this is a prime spot. Hyde Park is bigger and tends to attract more runners, at least on a weekend basis. Be aware though: Running in Hyde Park is a very humbling experience. For some reason, anyone who runs there is absolutely *rapid*. As I toured the lovely greenery at a seemingly comfortable pace, I often wondered if I was travelling backwards while a stampede of runners overtook me. Try not to pay attention to them as these places are prime training sports for the more seasoned athlete. Third is Victoria Park, which has just as nice scenery, but is let down by its one-way system, which *no-one* follows. Many runners as well as pedestrians are guilty of this. So, if you do ever run at Victoria Park, then let's try to set an example for public order and run in the direction of the arrows (please!).

Main task 2: Lunch, term 1 revision materials, dinner
Return from run/classes and cook a high-carb, high-protein lunch. Complete revision materials for each module. Dinner at 6:30pm. More carbs, more protein, and force-feed some beetroot. Return to work. Complete by 11:30pm, then go to bed.

Each meal was packed with energy, but that's about the only positive. I used to make tonnes of rice, cook a farm's worth of chicken, drown it in soy and Worcestershire sauce for a bit of flavour, and then allow a pack of beetroot to invade the dish and spew its violative purple juice all over the kitchen. Trust me, I can usually eat anything on a plate, but beetroot is absolutely off limits. I used to eat it raw and it would make me cringe and gag like a bad romcom. It was supposedly so healthy- good for clearing toxins in your stomach- so I pinched my nose and swallowed as quick as possible.

Work was frantic. I tried to juggle the current week's work with last term's, leaving no time to waste. No distractions were allowed as in-depth revision on previous topics could sometimes take up to four hours. With four modules to complete, I would be pushing eight-hour workdays. As the short days and long nights continued through the first weeks of 2017, I spent much of my time writing little revision flashcards at my desk, illuminated by my lava lamp.

By 11:30pm, I would be exhausted. I had done nothing but run and work all day. I would repeat the same tasks tomorrow, all the way up until everything was done. Did I find the large workload stressful? Not one bit. Was university still the lonely ordeal it was last term? I don't know, I hadn't been paying attention. I no longer cared. I was so infused in my work, in my little projects, and in my running that nothing else mattered. My goals took priority because I genuinely enjoyed working for them. I absolutely, without a doubt, hand on heart, proper bloody loved the grind.

Running was just getting better and better. My muscles were adapting, and my times were tumbling. I even allowed myself to purchase my first running shirt and shorts although mind you, being a student, those assets were acquired at Primark (not a running specialist, but still decent sportswear for the price). I felt like limits no longer applied to me. I was invincible. With this mindset, I could do anything as long as I consistently worked for it. In fact, I felt ready to up my mileage even before marathon training had begun! I had just completed an amazing 18-mile week, why not aim for 20?! Ambition surged through my veins.

Eventually, I completed Operation: Save Term 1 in grand style, finishing right on schedule. It was quickly followed by the announcement of my first ever university assignment result, which was a first-class grade on my first ever microeconomics paper. Having spent weeks fearing a low result, seeing my high mark which I achieved after what had largely been six weeks of imposter syndrome in the economics department, I have never celebrated a single grade as much in my life. I screamed in excitement like a delirious football fan, jumping around the room before I had to calm myself down with a cup of tea. As I boiled the kettle, I gazed out at the same busy road opposite the halls and viewed the nocturnal city in a different light. For the first time I viewed it as somewhere I can fit in and thrive. For the first time, I acknowledged that I deserved to be there. This was it. This was the big turnaround, and I was achieving it on my own accord.

Running was a constant motivator in achieving my daily goals. Once home, the runner's high made me excited to hit the books again. Running was teaching me that huge things were achievable by putting in the right work in the short-term, with each effort fitting together like a jigsaw. This positive cycle of motivation made me fearless. I figured that finally, I was learning how to become a functioning adult.

Unbounded ambition

After a hectic fortnight, rest was not on the agenda. The end of Operation: Save Term 1 did not feel like a signal to slow down, but an invitation to speed up. I would put my current running efforts to the test by attempting 8 miles, a distance I had never before covered in my whole life. I considered anything above 6 miles a large distance, so this would be a true test of my body's limits. During those 8 miles- which required eighteen tours around Russell Square Gardens- I felt my body reaching new levels of physical performance as I edged closer to my limit. As fatigue crept in, mental mantras propelled me forward. I welcomed all physical pain because I knew this was where I would learn just how much mental strength I really have.

As I ran with increased struggle, I reminded myself of the purpose of this very run and how it would contribute to the end goal. I reminded myself of how beneficial it will be when I soon start marathon training. Most importantly, I urged myself to keep moving forward, as every step covered was a success.

After coaching my aching limbs through the 8-mile distance, I sat in the halls' courtyard afterwards revelling in satisfaction. I had just gone beyond my limits and it felt *amazing*. What was next? There was an abundance of time to get on top of my studies and use this productivity to continue earning high grades. Nothing could stop me- my progress was exponential bruv.

I rested in bed that night knowing that in the past fortnight I had completed a whole term's worth of work, smashed my running records, and achieved an astonishingly high mark on one of my essays. I slept very well indeed. For once, in a very long time, I was in a state of content. I felt calm about the future and about university in general. While I may still be the campus loner, that no longer bothered me because I had found my personal drive as a university student. Everything was coming together on this path of self-discovery with running already proving to be a miracle worker. It seemed to be the perfect cure to my problems, at least from its short-term prospects. But as the famous saying goes, if it's too good to be true, it usually is.

I suspect many runners have experienced a similarly euphoric story when they first began, perhaps maybe not as drastic. As you can see, running really was like magic. It was the terminator of excuses, ego, and laziness and led me to believe that anything was possible with the right graft. However, the higher the rise, the greater the fall. It turns out, I had been digging myself into a hole the entire fortnight.

Could you spot the underlying flaws? We'll explore them in the next chapter to create a list of Do's and Don'ts for new runners. Let's just say for the time being that I was guilty of every Don't possible. Two days after my barrier-breaking 8-miles, I set out to run my first 6 miles of the week, with the hope to make the next two runs in the same week both 8-milers. As usual, I got my kit on, laced up my shoes, set my timer, and set off, not bothered at all by the unfamiliar aches concentrated in my left ankle; I just interpreted them as pains to overcome as a further challenge; they would eventually fade while running anyway.

But they didn't fade. They grew worse. Walking up the back alley felt unusually uncomfortable. The aches were sharper than usual in my left ankle. Still though, they'll surely subside once I'm running, right? I broke into a run. Uncomfortable for sure; 'Just get through it,' I thought, 'this is probably the hardest part.' Chants of, 'Don't stop!' from a Morning Musume song blasting through my headphones encouraged me to continue, even though the pain in my ankle was now strangely growing in anger, like a nail being hammered through the bone. I approached the end of the street as the song cheered 'Let's go!' but I had already stopped. I clutched the now piercing pain in my ankle- ouch.

Part Two: Lessons

Chapter 5
The one mistake every new runner makes

'This surely isn't happening,' I was freaking out. There I stood like a statue at the end of the road- reality had dealt its first paralysing blow since the epiphany. My left ankle screamed at me. Any attempt to apply pressure sent shockwaves of pain through the bone on the anterior side. Even attempts to walk slapped me with heaps of discomfort.

The sensation was entirely new, but I refused to believe the pain would be too much to continue. Perhaps this was the next hurdle I had to overcome? Maybe this was the kind of pain I had to learn to run through? After all, up to this point it was all just mental eustress without too much strain. Surely then, this was the next big challenge, right?

I took my headphones off and gritted my teeth in an attempt to press on through the pain. After all, to surpass my limit required defeating discomfort, right? Oh the horrifically agonising irony.

I stupidly tried to continue, despite my body's increased yells to quit and go home. I ran a further two streets before conceding to the fact that my face had already shrivelled up into a wincing grimace from ignoring the agony. I also ran lopsided, which probably didn't look too attractive from a distance. Finally, I halted to a standstill. *We've got a huge problem here.* I knew that continuing could be a dangerous decision; this acute pain might only get worse. It was just the idea of turning back and returning home. I didn't want to concede, I didn't want to give in.

For five whole minutes I stood frozen in place, contemplating my dilemma. I repeatedly applied pressure to the sensitive side of my ankle, pointlessly attempting to calculate a specific angle in which the pain wouldn't be so harsh. I planned to do 6 miles but couldn't even manage six steps pain-free. Who was I kidding? Time to face facts Ellis- you're clearly injured.

Now obviously common sense and sound logic tells us that when injured to the point where even gentle walking becomes painful, abandoning the run and going home is both the sensible and correct thing to do. But back then I did not appreciate this. Each ginger step back towards the halls made me feel like a failure. All that good work up to this point, all that I had planned- everything now fell into jeopardy. Can you believe that? Something was going wrong! An unexpected hiccup, a black swan in my master plan! How could this be possible? I thought I had planned the entire future day by day- I just didn't get it. It's almost like I completely forgot that in the real world, plans rarely- if ever- run smoothly from start to finish.

I moped back to my room, jumped on my bed and propped the ankle in question up on the desk chair for inspection. The pain was in the bony area on the inside, the bit that sticks out, if we're being precise. The pain could only be described as very sharp and sensitive to pressure. Panic set in. I was bed bound and now devoid of my superpower. What was I going to do? What exactly was this injury and how long would it take to heal? My mind accelerated into overdrive and I bordered on experiencing a panic attack. Marathon training was due to begin *next week*. The whole point of these pre-training runs was to bring me up to speed and establish a good baseline going into the real programme- that had horribly backfired.

Now, I was unable to run at all and the possibility that I wouldn't be fit to even begin the first week became worryingly real. Suddenly, the first week- which I so confidently remarked that I could already do- looked beyond my capabilities, given the state of my ankle. I may have planned months in advance for marathon success, but I was already looking at falling behind schedule before training had even started.

Mental meltdown

No, no, no- everything was going wrong! The plans were falling apart just like the tendons in my ankle. I couldn't gather my thoughts together after dejectedly typing the word 'injured' into my running log. I had never envisioned such a setback, not least this early on. In my short running career of a few weeks, I thought I had gotten it all right. I thought I had steadied myself but pushed when needed. I thought the mileage was building up wonderfully, putting me in pole position to cruise through the first weeks of training. It was such a mystery. I didn't even remember landing awkwardly on my ankle at any point at all!

Such was the naivete of teenage Ellis who had only ever experienced acute injuries in his life.

The dull pain behind my ankle now growled with a sharp stabbing sensation, which throbbed as I lay on my bed, propping it on the desk chair. *What to do, what to do...* I had nothing to treat it and no clue on what it needed- my aim was to learn how to run, not how to treat injuries! I leant over and grabbed my phone to begin a streak of Google searches that would give conflicting clues as to what was wrong. In a matter of minutes, I learnt various vocabulary about the anatomy of the ankle and the various potential problems that arise with tendons. I learnt of horrible conditions and syndromes- all of which hinted at an extended period of months away from running- alongside hefty rehab routines and permanent problems with my foot. I didn't want to believe any of them so each time I re-diagnosed myself with a slightly kinder condition. The process continued for over an hour.

I scrutinised my ankle constantly by pressing, rubbing, and occasionally smacking, to test out its sensitivity. Even though the pain was so concentrated, the source of its rage felt further below the surface than initially thought. I attempted to walk up and down in my 6-metre long room to gauge which part of the running motion was causing the most disturbance. It turned out that pushing through the ball of my foot, as you do for forward momentum, was the source of my troubles.

Every website I visited, every YouTube video watched, and every forum read, all initially suggested icing the damaged area, propping it up, and resting it for a while.[4] I thought that if I wanted a quick fix then I had to act fast, and maybe by icing it while the pain was still raw that could speed up the recovery process. I had no ice though- time to get creative.

I rummaged around my top draw, pulled out a freezer bag, and then proceeded to hop to the kitchen like a proper diva to reach a tap. Holding onto the wall for balance, I did all I could to prevent my left foot from touching the floor as if it were lava. Once in the kitchen, I filled the bag with water and placed it in the freezer. As I peered into the top compartment, a strange but practical idea popped into my head.

The logical object to acquire was of course ice, but that was only because it was freezing cold to soothe the pain. As such, anything that was freezing cold in my freezer would do, wouldn't it? Well, I was in desperate need of a quick fix and thus resorted to anything I could find. I explored the freezer, consciously avoiding the second drawer- where someone spilt some kind of liquid before Christmas and now Narnia's growing out of it- and eventually chose a large and already opened bag of oven chips. 'It's better than nothing,' I thought to myself as I brought the bag back to my room. I lay back down on the bed and positioned the chair closer before taking out the chips one by one and placing them

---

[4] The common routine is called 'RICE', and rather than resting your foot in rice for an evening and hoping it works afterwards, the acronym stands for 'Rest', 'Ice', 'Compression', and 'Elevation'.

around the bony point of my ankle. It was quite intricate; I stacked each chip like they were Jenga blocks and eventually had a small covering of frozen chips on my foot.

They produced somewhat of a cooling sensation, but then again, they also produced a lot of grease. Plus, I had to remain fixed in position so they didn't fall onto the carpet, but also hope that they didn't thaw too quickly. For fifteen minutes I lay still and browsed the web for more online wisdom.

I began to notice patterns in my 'research'. The term 'sprain' often cropped up, and further down the page would be the term 'stress fracture'. With the two injury culprits following me around the internet I felt complied to match myself with one. After all, every search term and subsequent webpage viewed would lead me to those two; through the art of deduction I felt like I was homing in on my true diagnosis.

As any rational human being would, I tried to frame the entire situation as if it were merely a sprain. A sprain suggested a minor acute trauma, requiring a few days rest before a return to action. I had minor sprains in my wrists before, so perhaps this was just the same but for the ankle. Stress fractures sounded too scary to entertain; the thought of one of my bones cracking under the repeated dollop of energy pressing through my feet sounded horrible. And such an injury would side-line me not just for weeks, but *months*. No, it couldn't be a fracture.

Surely it was just a sprain? It's probably just a common pain! In fact, there was plenty of YouTube content to bolster my chances of a speedy recovery. One guy seemed to know it all, promising pain relief within twenty-four hours with his 'special' ankle routine which differs from the traditional ankle injury treatments; he believed his discovery to be so valuable he bundled it into a £50 eBook! I won't name such clowns- even I wasn't silly enough to fall for those scams back then. A word of warning: much like the 'gurus' who promise 'financial freedom', there are also similar figures who want to profit off your desperation for a quick solution. Let's not fall for them. I'll be honest, I gave his deal a fair bit of thought, knowing full well my desire to not miss a single running session. Luckily, my student-esque stinginess won out in the end and my wallet remained safe.

As I raced through each video explaining how to heal a sprained ankle, doubts began to gain traction in my mind. The symptoms spoke of restricted motion and bruising, caused by a single moment in which the ankle underwent trauma. I had no recollection of this happening to me, nor did I feel as if any bruising would develop. I could also move my ankle fine, it was just placing pressure on it, placing pressure on the *bone* that produced pain. Oh no… I felt myself gradually succumbing to the fears that maybe this injury was much worse than feared. Maybe I *had* fractured my ankle. Maybe the London streets had wrecked my feet and reduced them to rubble. The soft soil of the countryside which caressed each step seemingly lured my body into a false sense of security. The switch to concrete must have been the killer blow, surely.

After all, it couldn't have been *me*, no! I was running healthily at my limit, never pushing too hard for too long and instead making gradual gains in fitness and endurance- wasn't I? Regardless, it was my problem for the unforeseeable future, and I had no idea what to do. Maybe I would be unable to run for months. Maybe I wouldn't be able to train for the marathon. Maybe the recovery would take so long that I would have to postpone my marathon challenge to next year. Oh the horror! I lay back with my head sinking into the pillow and ran a hand through my hair as I contemplated the dark scenarios confronting me. I stressed and panicked and fretted at an issue which my mind had no control over; it was up to my body to heal itself.

The dramatic slump

All this worrying was exhausting. The week had gotten off to the worst possible start. The dread of the long road to recovery ahead consumed all thinking space. Running had become such an essential element of everyday life and with it ripped away, I became unable to focus on anything else that mattered. My productivity properly plummeted. For the rest of the day, I could not spare a single thought for whatever university work I had to do. I just lay on my bed frantically Googling injury diagnoses and estimated recovery times. I spent the whole night worrying, pinning my hopes on waking up with a healed foot.

When the low sun breathed life back into the morning, I would walk a few steps up and down my room and cautiously comfort myself with the optimism that the injury had magically vanished after a few painless steps. I would press down gently on the ball of my foot and the pain wouldn't growl so harshly. I would then push harder, only to then receive the angry response that I so feared. I attempted to then cover up the continued presence of the injury by convincing myself it had only been so sore because I pressed hard and fast onto the floor- 'It's better than yesterday' became a mantra.

But soon you become weary of convincing yourself that 'just one more day of rest' will be enough and accept that you're only feeding yourself false hope. The recovery is never as quick as we hope. My productivity slumped, as did my mood- I felt low, very low. *I'm scheduled to run today- I need to run today!* All I wanted to do was run, but that simple pleasure had been taken away. Work suffered as a result. Now, none of my revision materials looked any good and they took longer to complete. It all felt pointless and aimless once again. I didn't have that ambitious desire to work anymore; I wanted this injury fixed now! I could no longer concentrate in classes; I sat in the corner and uttered not a single word, spending the entire time stewing over my injury crisis. It occupied my mind so much that even in the small talk before tutorials I found a way to shoehorn my woes into every single conversation with complete strangers- I lost all social awareness by being trapped in the chaos of my mind. The whole ordeal had completely rocked my equilibrium; my one source of hope, my only access to fulfilment... was gone.

Training was now on the ropes. It was all going wrong, all fading away. Everything I had gained and achieved since the beginning of the year- was it just a fad, like a New Year's resolution which had lost its novelty and glamour? No, this was different; I just wanted to run. That's all I needed. I didn't want to do anything else. Without running, my motivation had deserted me, and I was depressed again.

The Do's and Don'ts for when you start running

Oh deary me- it's all gone horribly wrong, hasn't it? I hope you're not surprised to read that my running career quickly fell into this pit of doom. If you're surprised at all, then it's a good thing you're reading this chapter, otherwise you're at risk of ending up like this sorry sack of pity I found myself in back then. I hope chronicling the spectacular slump that followed my injury has provided an unnerving example of what can happen to the beginner runner should they make the one critical mistake that I did (if not, then the next chapter should hopefully get you).

You may be wondering, what was that critical mistake? But the chances are you're already aware. It's no complicated matter yet it's something that most new runners do not take into account, and even for experienced runners it is something we're all guilty of every now and then. When it comes to running as a beginner, the biggest mistake you can ever make is overdoing it.

I did not know exactly what was wrong with my ankle, and as you'll soon read, I had many headaches trying to diagnose the injury. But, regardless of what went wrong, it's a pretty safe bet that the cause was overuse of the ligaments which eventually could not bear the repeated stress any longer. When looking back at my running log for the first three weeks of January, it is no surprise that something like this happened. On the first week I ran two sessions lasting 4.5 miles, which was actually not too bad. They were suitably separated by a couple of days, allowing my muscles to recover. Where all strayed wrong was immediately after the epiphany, where reckless ambition then took over.

Once back in London, the dizzying skyscrapers and toxic polluted air must have done something to me, because all of a sudden I went from completing a couple of 4.5-milers in a week to running 6-milers, three times in a week; this also came while I implemented an intensive study plan which left me hardly any room to breathe during the day. The 9 miles I ran in the first week of 2017 abruptly jumped to 18 the following week. I doubled my distance, reduced time taken to rest in between runs, extended the length of those runs as well as the frequency, and to make it just a bit more ridiculous, tried to go at maximum speed each and every time- every run turned into a new PB attempt!

The following week was even more relentless with an 8-mile run at the end; I demanded more from myself every time, ignorant to the fact my body was not physically capable of the workload I was forcing it through yet. I thought I understood the idea of gradual improvements but failed horribly at implementing it in practice. Hindsight is a wonderful thing, but honestly, back then I became hooked on the idea that my progress could only climb higher and higher as everything fell perfectly into place.

There were further mistakes that need to be mentioned. Running 0.3-mile laps around Russell Square Gardens was a recipe for disaster in itself. With overuse the primary detriment, imagine running around the same course eighteen times non-stop? If you run lapped courses, then the biggest issue to be aware of is the ground's camber, which is the slant at the sides of each surface you run on. This is an issue found more on uneven rural roads but exists almost everywhere; it's unlikely you will ever complete a run entirely on perfectly flat roads. By running with your ankles at a constant angle, you compromise your biomechanics by placing extra stress on one side. It was therefore no coincidence that the ankle which became injured was the one constantly smashing the ground at an unnatural angle.

As we've seen up to this point, running can be a source of huge inspiration and motivation in your early days; for me, the combination of the runner's high and the prospect of completing a marathon roughly around the same time as my first year exams set me up for a Hollywood finish, thus spurring me into dangerous levels of productivity. I say dangerous because it was simply not sustainable. Running is a powerful mood-regulator and developer of willpower, but blowing your load like me in the space of two weeks will leave you feeling burnt out and inevitably injured.

If there is one thing we should all remember, whether beginner or Olympian, is that when it comes to challenging ourselves, our body is never as enthusiastic as our minds may be. I'm a prime example- my mind wanted to go further and faster each and every session, but my body was simply not capable of that rapid progression. Bodies are simply rational reactors to irrational minds, hence the overuse injuries. So that's partly why we train, to bring our body up to the expectations of the mind.

Therefore, it is vital as part of our building of self-discipline to learn how to moderate our energy expenditure. More specifically, with running we must learn how to exert ourselves through sensible distances and speeds which respect our physical limits and current levels of fitness. The first step in moderating our weekly mileage levels is to learn and respect the 10% rule: Never increase your mileage by more than 10% over the previous week.

Let's use an example of a runner who starts off with a baseline of 15 miles a week. With the 10% rule, their distance for the following week should be no more than 16.5 miles. While this may seem frustratingly slow, realise that you will already be running over 30 miles weekly after just eight weeks. Recalling my previous example, I went from 9 miles in a week to 18, henceforth an increase of 100%. No wonder I got injured then, eh? So remember, this is a part of the long-term, gradual adaptation process that is key to becoming a successful runner. It may seem overly cautious, but it will result in huge gains in the long run.

With that in mind, let's make a note of the following list. So far in this book we've talked about inspirations, how to equip yourself for the first run, and how to go about your exciting first few adventures on the open roads. We've seen the explosive euphoria which propelled me into unprecedented levels of self-belief and productivity, all possible for any soul that becomes addicted to the runner's high, and now we have seen that hit a brick wall with injury. So, before we progress into dealing with injuries and maturing as a runner, let's consolidate the key bullet points for those starting out, aimed at both new runners and those starting a new training regime, because the runner's high can inflate our ambitions regardless of experience level:

The DO's:
- DO ensure you wear comfortable clothes and shoes that fit you
- DO warm up before each session with dynamic stretching, and warm down with both dynamic and static stretching afterwards
- DO start off gentle and run your 'tune up' runs at a comfortable pace, enough to maintain a conversation
- DO adhere to the 10% rule
- DO trust in the process of gradual adaptation and remain faithful to your training plan
- DO be mindful of the difference between discomfort (muscle fatigue) and pain (injury)

The DON'Ts:
- DON'T run every session like you're going for a new PB
- DON'T push for personal best distances before a month of steady running
- DON'T run the same course repeatedly; mix up your route
- DON'T increase your mileage by more than 10% each week
- DON'T compare yourself to other runners
- DON'T go above and beyond your training plan just because you feel capable of more

To make sure you fulfil each of these points requires a sound knowledge of yourself and your own body. You have to run to *your* limits, not someone else's. Your competitive flame may begin roaring if overtaken when out for a run or when you see a plethora of proud faces effortlessly smashing it on Instagram. The key is to develop your self-discipline and realise that the decision to go beyond your comfort zone must also gain approval from your own body. If you're feeling sharp pains, or tight and tired muscles, then usually that is a sign to focus on rest and recovery for a bit- there is no clearer sign than muscle or tendon inflammation which, as it turns out, was precisely the issue I faced. Inflammation is your body's natural reaction to being overstressed and thus you should take its advice- inflammation only becomes a chronic problem if you aggravate the issue further.

Indeed, the primary requirement to enjoy a successful start to your running career is self-discipline, because as I have proven, running can make you delusional with euphoria in the early stages. Don't get me wrong, it's fantastic to feel on top of the world, to feel your best self, and to feel capable of surpassing any challenge you place on yourself. But remember that Rome wasn't built in a day and likewise the greatest *you* won't be constructed after one run. To enjoy running well into old age, you must bear in mind that it is a long-term project. So, the PBs can wait and so can the mileage records. They *will* come, but only when your body knows the time is right.

Next, a reminder: If you follow all these rules, then there is still a chance you can pick up an injury while running. The fact is our bodies can be unpredictable and react differently to all kinds of new situations. You may not be so in tune with your body when you begin running (as I have proved), which in itself presents a risk. Yet, no matter how well you know your body and no matter how well you train, you will most likely get an injury at some point. It's just inevitable. But, by following these rules, you can avoid becoming one of those miserable people who have to deal with a new injury every week. You might even become a runner who has mastered the art of stretching, post-run recovery, and managing your energy expenditure to live a life largely injury-free.

And now, a word of advice: when injuries do inevitably crop up, you must know how to mentally deal with them so that their impact only slows your progression without reducing it. My mistake with my first injury revealed the extent of my undeveloped mental fortitude. I became obsessed with the damage to my plans that I completely overlooked the importance of maintaining my efforts (where possible) during the short term. My concerns on the long-term detriment to my marathon hopes spilt over to the short-term requirements for my university goal. I thus jeopardised myself in all areas.

You cannot do much to speed up the body's natural healing process with injuries, but you can speed up your mind's knowledge accumulation process drastically with this extra time. Thus, if you find yourself in a period where you are unable to run, then as a new runner, try to use the time to study stretching exercises; for example, yoga, nutrition, or anything related to running that will equip you with the skills and mindset to come back even stronger and wiser- this we will cover further in chapter 10. Don't forget as well that many runners will have been through the same ordeals, so learning from their recovery stories- plenty of which you can find in *Runner's World*- will also be a great source of reassuring inspiration.

So, how did I overcome this major blow to my plans? Was there really a stress fracture? Was I to be side-lined for the indefinite future? Was the marathon dream over? Well, as you can see there are plenty more pages in this book. Perhaps all of them are filled with my sob story from the crippling depression of not being able to run. Or maybe, there was light at the end of the tunnel. Or so I thought.

At the end of the day, while determination and resourcefulness can help pave the way for solutions, learning your lessons is the best way to prevent mistakes from reoccurring. Fail to learn from your past mistakes and the next time you repeat them the consequences may be far worse. The next chapter thus documents my lowest point in this entire journey.

Chapter 6
Injuries: Learn your lessons

If you don't learn from your injury lessons, then you are doomed to repeat them until you probably want to quit running. You are susceptible to this particularly if you tie your mood and productivity to being able to run, which was the exact mistake I made. Owing to injury, my schedule, mood, and productivity completely crashed. Those glory days where I could run any distance and any intensity pain-free seemed almost too good to be true... And that's because they were.

It's not possible to sustain the 100% jumps in mileage from week to week while spending every other minute of the day furiously working. By the end of Operation: Save Term 1, I was already beginning to feel burnt out. It's unsurprising, then, that my body decided to take matters into its own hands and eventually pull me out of action. There are few better signs of disconnect between mind and body than an overuse injury.

However, what may seem surprising is after all that drama and agony and despair in the last chapter, I was back running again in just one week. And no, it wasn't a miracle cure- all it took was a rest from the emphatic expectations I repeatedly placed on my body as my deliria (disguised as euphoria) inflated exponentially. Can you believe that? Who would've thought?

Many invaluable lessons were learned- or supposed to be learned- from this, both about myself and about how to deal with injuries. I first learnt that I was guilty of every Don't from our list in chapter 5, particularly with regards to overdoing it. I did not know my personal limits and forced my body way beyond its recognised comfort zone without enough rest- the inevitable injury therefore came as no surprise. I had become so absorbed in immediate gratification from running that I turned my back on the long-term, deferred gratification. This highlights the importance of remaining faithful to our training plans and letting the improvements come naturally, not when we impulsively fancy setting new personal records one after the other.

I also learnt that I had become dependent purely on the act of running, judging by how I ceased to function for seven days just because I couldn't complete a mere few runs. Allow me to properly explain because this is worth remembering. There is more to running than simply running; there is the community, the challenges, the events, the stories, and a vast and boundless realm of knowledge waiting to be discovered, whether that be training tips, nutritional advice, or the ground-breaking scientific breakthroughs through our sport that teach us vital and infinitely fascinating things about us as humans. Or, it's simpler things, like having a routine, or the excitement of thinking, 'One day I'm gonna do this'- 'this' being any personal milestone you wish, which in my case was a full marathon. I quickly fell in love with the sport for all these things; for the first time in months I had a passion again. Reading magazines, watching videos, and learning of humankind's great endeavours immersed me into a new and exciting world. Even when we're side-lined from running, that world is still accessible. Even without being able to run, there are so many aspects of the sport we can still enjoy and learn from.

To tie your mood entirely to the act of running is to put all your eggs in one basket. Thus, I couldn't allow not being able to run halt my university productivity ever again and vowed to become a student of the sport, not just a hyped fan. Just because the body is recovering doesn't mean we can't stimulate the mind.

Oh, and another important lesson learned: Don't ever attempt to self-diagnose on the internet- you'll probably convince yourself in the end that amputating your limbs is the only way, or at the very least, unintentionally end up feeling a whole lot worse about the situation. Consult a professional if your injury is something beyond requiring just a few days of rest.

Returning to running

To avoid reinjuring my ankle straight away, I took advice from *Runner's World* and equipped myself with shock-absorbing insoles and kinesiology tape. Insoles are a great purchase, particularly for city runners. They feature more rubber cushioning than the standard factory soles, which means your shoes will absorb greater amounts of energy from pounding the pavements, taking the shock away from your legs.

Kinesiology tape is also very helpful for muscle strains or aching areas. Research suggests it is beneficial for musculoskeletal pain, helping stimulate blood flow to inflamed areas.[5] It helped me comfortably return to 100% and I got to get creative with the many different colours available- by the time I had finished taping you could easily mistake me for a character from Tron.

When it comes to injury recovery products, always remember that our bodies are all unique and different from one another. What works for one person might not work for another. Don't go ahead with anything whacky like submerging yourself in ice for three days to treat inflammation, or tasering your feet with 1000 volts in hopes of 'stimulating' the nerves. And always consult a professional for more serious problems.

It must not be ignored that the best way to deal with injuries, particularly overuse ones, is to of course avoid getting them altogether. By following the list in the previous chapter and learning what your body is telling you, you will be able to run smarter, which does not necessarily entail running harder. If you feel tired or have a few sharp pains, then rest. If a pain lingers, see it as a sign to lower the intensity. Use a bit of long-term thinking- it's better to sacrifice a couple of runs in the week if it means you avoid being hoisted onto a physiotherapy table for three months.

---

[5] Lim, E.C. and M.G. Tay, *Kinesio taping in musculoskeletal pain and disability that lasts for more than 4 weeks: is it time to peel off the tape and throw it out with the sweat? A systematic review with meta-analysis focused on pain and also methods of tape application.* Br J Sports Med, 2015. 49(24): p. 1558-66.

So, with all this wisdom in mind, do you think I learnt my lessons and skipped off merrily into the sunset to complete marathon training? Of course not. I only injured myself again the very next week, didn't I.

Repeating the same mistakes

Hallelujah bitches- I'm back. I thought myself the recipient of many blessings- not only could I begin the training plan on time, but I could also bin my own running schedule, the one which almost fractured my ankle.

Wrapped up tight in kinesiology tape to be on the safe side and supported by multiple layers of rubber cushioning under my feet, I boldly embarked out into the sharp January air with an inferno of motivation burning bright inside of me. 'This is where it all comes together,' I spoke to myself while beginning the 10-minute walk as instructed by the training plan. After that I would run at an easy pace for 20 minutes, and then conclude the session with a 5-minute walk. Nice and straightforward, no problems at all- I completed the session with my lungs still intact and no aches or pains in any region of my body. The run definitely did not push me to my limit but that wasn't the aim. I returned home delighted knowing I had completed the first run of the 17-week plan exactly as it advised. Now all I had to do was return to work, rest the next day, and then go about my business again, repeating until we arrived at the start-line in May.

It all seemed so simple didn't it? But alas, my inexperience added unnecessary complications which turned out to be detrimental. The first week was sublime- every session was completed as per the plan and I looked to be on track to slowly build my fitness up to marathon standard. Yet, once again, the act of running within my physical endeavours was the only aspect I dedicated my focus towards amidst competition for time from university. As such, the required 'core and stretching' for every Friday took a backseat while I focussed on university work. For the same reason, my warm-ups became part of the walking segments in each session while the warm downs consisted merely of the short walk through reception. If I just about managed to get away with that laziness in the easy first few weeks, then rest assured (in every sense), it would bite hard later with increased mileage.

That laziness did indeed have consequences and this time I paid a proper price. Another injury- only this time considerably more painful, with a longer recovery time, and undoubtedly one of the most notorious injuries in the running world.

We begin our disaster with just one week left of term before 'reading week', which is basically a week's break. I powered through each run but never bothered with a single stretch. The only thing I tried to stretch was time; my plan of creating revision materials for each week's lecture topics created much work to do during the evenings and thus corners were cut. I planned to get all of this week's and last week's content completed so that I could enjoy a break back home guilt-free. To give you a bit of detail, that two weeks' worth of content equated to three 20-page textbook chapters producing roughly 75 hand-written flashcards. And that's for one module. Multiply that amount by four and you have the workload for all modules. That's a right bloody load of reading and writing.

With the work seemingly endless, my motivation and enthusiasm started to peter out. I started to wake up later, bargaining that an extra 10-minute lie-in would grant the energy to get all my tasks done. 10 minutes turned into an hour, and then with meal prep factored in, all my daily tasks started competing for time. Everything became a rush. Everything had to be done but there just were not enough hours in the day. A sense of dread that I wasn't getting enough done gradually grew; the pressure and anxiety bred procrastination, which only made matters worse as each day I took longer and longer to start my tasks.

Everything felt like a chore. It was just a scramble to complete everything that had to be completed- I had unknowingly let running turn into another obligation- another obligation which I did not feel motivated as much as before. *Why do I do this to myself? Why do I have to charge in all guns blazing, only to run out of ammo and then allow myself to get shot down?*

Each run just felt like a case of going out and getting the damn task completed. It was completion or failure- I was too tired and grumpy to see it any other way- regardless of the fact that my legs, particularly the knees, were feeling really lethargic. A dull ache sat behind my kneecap, not growling, but purring enough to alert me of its presence. I knew full well that my body was not in ideal condition ahead of another week of training. But I also believed that I was capable of completing the upcoming sessions while the aches were of no serious concern. What would you do in this situation? I would hope that- at the very least- the intelligent runner would know to ease off, if not take the session off altogether. Teenage Ellis, on the other hand, decided to go for it anyway, once again ignoring the fact that small aches can turn into long-term chronic injuries.

And just as you have come to expect, I went and got myself injured- again. Eventually my knee decided, 'Right, I can't do this anymore mate,' and as I sat back in my chair after a mid-week interval session, it began building a fort of inflammation. The area around the kneecap stiffened and that dull pain became an agitated snarl. I immediately clocked I had sustained a second injury, but this time did not panic- I now had the tools and experience to recover quickly- I'll be back out there in a week!

Being back at the family home meant I had access to ice from the freezer, with a nice stool to prop my knee up. But after 15 minutes of icing, the pain transitioned from a sharp stabbing sensation to a nasty grinding stiffness. As a passing note, I also realised that I had been icing my knee not with water, but chicken stock, thus forcing me to immediately run a bath and purify myself from the stinky substance. Inside the tub I contemplated the pain and began convincing myself once again that the injury was only minor and would not disrupt the next session.

Rock bottom

The injury cycle had begun again. Like before, attempts to run while carrying an obvious injury did get me any further than the end of the road. Another run aborted; back to lying on my bed and going through the stages of denial.

The typical injury cycle unfolds as follows: You start out by downplaying the injury as only a tiny niggle, which with moderate rest would allow for a return to action in the next scheduled session. Then, upon awakening each morning you test the injured area, and swiftly confirm to yourself that the pain has definitely died down and dismiss any subsequent rush of raw intense pain as simply an anomaly. However, the real test of actually running always delivers the most unwelcome reality check: the injury is no better than before and requires much more rest than you're willing to take.

If you're me, then additional stages involve afternoons of repeated Google searches (as far as page 2) and attempts to self-diagnose, only to reach a false conclusion due to confirmation bias- I would only consider injuries that had a short recovery time, anything over two weeks went into the mental filing cabinet labelled, 'Nah that's definitely not it, and even if it is, it's not.'

Once I returned to London after a week with the obsolete knee, the same depressive slump as before followed. This time however, it was even more pitiful than before; the sort that makes you want to scribble an anthology's worth of emo poetry. I began to doubt whether I really could be a runner. Forget the marathon- *can I even run? Perhaps the injuries are a sign. Perhaps I've been fooling myself this whole time. A marathon, really?* Perhaps all those years of embarrassment at cross country and Sunday league football were enough evidence that running just wasn't my forte. Maybe that 'bold' decision to sign up for a marathon was just a delusional episode. And university? *Come on, you were never academic at school, were you? You just had a good memory.* This was real work now. Memorising textbooks might not get me very far anymore.

So many destructive doubts. And then there were the next five weeks, which would be enough to set anyone's anxiety alight. Three essays and two presentations to complete in three weeks- the pressure was truly on now. I thought of how I so desperately wished running could motivate me through the intense workload. I thought of how I craved the motivation to get me through the stress. Without it, I began to seriously reconsider my standing at university. The imposter syndrome was mitigated by running, but now I once again felt unworthy. I thought I had bitten off more than I could chew with both running and this degree.

After two weeks of rest, I already figured that my hopes of continuing marathon training were slipping. I *needed* to be able to run again, but a failed treadmill run at the gym was a reminder that this knee would not heal straight away. It was the most soul-crushing moment: I stepped onto the treadmill with the most intense hope that after a fortnight of refraining from running I would at last move pain-free. Imagine two weeks all leading up to one moment, but then you feel the exact same pain which confirms that your absolute worst-case scenario remains a reality. I wanted to scream and cry and curse the world for teasing me that

INJURIES: LEARN YOUR LESSONS

I could somehow conquer my mental demons at university. The nightmare continued.

A couple of weeks resting would not be enough to recover because I had the infamous 'runner's knee', or 'patellofemoral pain syndrome' as the doctors call it. It was another overuse injury (surprise, surprise) caused by a weakening of the patella (front area of the knee) after prolonged periods of stress (oops).

A complicated road to recovery lied ahead as my knee was susceptible to sharp pain wherever I tried to travel. Walking hurt and sitting with it bent during lectures for two hours also hurt. Henceforth, I attempted to change the way I walk and sit. While sitting with one leg out in front of me completely straight gave the image of an improperly postured delinquent, walking in a way that involved twisting my whole leg throughout the swinging motion, rather than bending it at the knee like one normally does, made me look like a right plonker- I recall one girl giving me very strange eyes when I passed her with my leg spinning around like it had a screw loose. My eyes are up here, darlin'.

It didn't matter what specialist equipment I chucked money at- there was no overnight cure. I tried a knee support, but if anything, it was counterproductive- I had it on so tight during an economics class that I had to bounce around on my one usable leg afterwards like I was on a bloody pogo stick. The equipment was failing and with each attempt to run again I only felt worse. Staff at all the sports shops shrugged their shoulders when I mentioned my knee and the doctor said to continue resting- no one had concrete answers nor an estimated recovery time and it pissed me off immensely because this living hell just did not seem to end.

Perhaps this was the true signal that running just wasn't for me. My motivation to continue working had long deserted me at this point and after two weeks of no running, I lay on my bed reflecting on how everything was ruined. Surely now it was too late to resume my training plan after missing two crucial weeks. I let out a long melancholic sigh, and with a shake of my head, whimpered, 'Running just isn't for me.'

Refusing to fail

But then I sat up. I looked down at my knee, and then looked at myself in the mirror. I realised I was in London, living on my own, paying premium prices to achieve an objective. Yet, I allowed myself to remain dejected and constantly wallowing by deciding I was never suited to running, nor university itself. Anger brewed.

'So what's the solution then? Just accept you're pathetic and go home?' I yelled before crashing back down onto the pillow, 'You little bitch.'

Now, one thing I want to make very clear: I did not feel any ounce of motivation, only disappointment and anger.

'No! Running *isn't* for you! It never was! But don't you bloody see- that's exactly why you started!'

When the going gets tough, always remember your reasons. Right now, they spoke to me clearer and more amplified than ever before. This whole time, the reason I had started to stumble was me. *I* was the one talking myself out of both running and university the whole time.

'Running's hard and university is a load of rubbish. What else do you want me to tell you, that the Pope's catholic?' I shot out of bed and began marching around my room. I often did this during sixth form- I would walk in circles around my room half ranting, half giving myself a pep talk. For the first time in a while I gave myself some tough love- I wasn't getting mad, I was getting even.

'You can go on moaning about how terrible everything is, how hard your life is, and how difficult it is to run with injuries and study while stressed. But the reality is no one gives a shit. Everyone's struggling in their own ways, fighting their own battles. The people who are always comfortable are the ones who never achieve anything! I'm sure you'd love to go back to Medway and live the small inconsequential life you had in school, but it's over, it's finished. Everyone's moved on. *This* is your life now.'

By now I was fiercely staring myself down in the mirror. For a split second I wondered if my next-door neighbour could hear me rambling like a sergeant.

'You may not like it, but this is the way things are. Uni will be a slog and running will be a battle with injuries unless you learn to stop galloping around like a lunatic with every opportunity. You can't change any of this. And don't back out and quit either, because then you *will* be a failure. The thought of it seems scary, dunnit? Passing first year, running the marathon… Do you really believe you can't do it? I don't think you do. I think you genuinely believe you *can* run 26.2 miles, but that's probably the easy part- try getting to the start line first! That's obviously the bigger challenge at the moment, eh? Remember: you made a choice; this is the reality of that choice. No use backing out now! You have time. Lots of it even. Use it or lose it. Lying on top of your bed in a sulk because you're not getting your own way? That's definitely time wasted, you little wasteman. Work with what you've got, almost anything would be better than scrolling up and down B-grade memes on Instagram.'

Sounds a bit like a drama when the main character confronts a physical version of their own conscience, doesn't it? I'm just being honest. Running, university, and anything worth accomplishing for that matter, can be psychological warfare sometimes. During that time of my life, I had no mentor, no one I felt I could rely on, and no example to follow, so I had to be honest with myself because no one else would. The fact is, I had been a whiny little brat who wanted everything straight away. I wanted everything to always go my own way. Life isn't like that. You have to make things work for you. In a way, you have to make your own luck.

Hence why we must learn to persevere through the tough times if we want to enjoy the good times. This is the true challenge when training for a marathon and training for life in general. It would be easy to give up and quit, return to our normal and dissatisfied lives, and just forget all about it by accepting that it is what it is. After all, I never told anyone I would be running a marathon, right? But still, I would be letting myself down, knowing that I gave up, just like with football- I would give up and fail again. I would be back to square one.

Once again, you always a choice: accept your problems or work through them. The latter is hard, because you have to deal with so many setbacks, both physical, mental, and sometimes financial to achieve it. If something really is worthwhile, then it inevitably will throw up doubts and numerous trials to attain it. If you're not willing to put up with that then you have no chance of breaking through your problems as you would passively be allowing them to trample all over you. If I wasn't willing to continue with recovering from my injury and give up, then the marathon and university dream would be dead, not because of my injury, but because I chose to stop trying.

Even with the setbacks, even in your darkest hour - you're still in the game. You haven't lost by any means. As long as you keep going, then the chances are you're probably still closer to winning. The marathon was still waiting in May and I was still enrolled on my four-year degree. Work was still in progress and time was still in abundance. I just had to get my arse in gear.

The big lesson

Explosively high levels of motivation were what drove me to complete those initial intense runs and workloads. But the problem with sudden strong bursts of motivation is the dramatic drop in energy once it eventually leaves you. You're left with the expectation to keep up the massive workloads and hate yourself when you no longer have that same energy to continue.

It's a bit like drinking a coffee, powering through your tasks, and then feeling drained once the caffeine wears off. The energy you receive from motivation is finite, and after so many successive influxes of motivation the length of the psychological boost shortens and your mind and body become borderline immune to it. After so many coffees your body becomes numb to the caffeine rush and thus the boost disappears, doesn't it? The two are alike- the façade gradually fades.

Overall, if we're being frank, operating throughout life purely through coffee and motivation probably isn't so sustainable- one might give you a heart attack, the other will leave you (quite literally) feeling very burnt out. And that summed me up as we approached February; I was pretty damn exhausted and as such the motivation and energy to complete my tasks began to fizzle out, opening the door for the familiar habit of procrastinating by scrolling through my social media feeds to return.

It's not bad to feel motivated, motivation itself gives us a reason and a terrific giddy excitement to go out and kick arse. But, it's not good to let short-term bursts of it set an unattainable long-term standard of performance. We must not be greedy and bite off more than we can chew, or risk chundering everything you've devoured up to that very point.

Whether you let motivation drive you to extremes or not, when times inevitably get tough it's likely going to run away from you. And let's be real- we don't know what our motivation will do in the future anyway, do we? It could go up, down, sideways, anywhere- the important thing is we learn to carry on to completion regardless of what our motivation is doing.

Step forward, willpower: the stoic driver that will pull us from our deepest of ruts and propel us into continuing to take action. This is what separates the dreamers from the doers. From now on, we toss aside motivation- we are no longer concerned about it. We made a choice and set a goal which despite hitting an obstacle, is a goal still very much in progress. And so, we turn our attention to developing willpower and going beyond what the volatility of the mind dictates. In doing so, we find that we can edge closer towards our goals even through setbacks.

Chapter 7
Willpower: The key to sustained success

When life pushes you down, you must get up. As the Japanese saying 七転び八起き goes, 'Fall down seven times, get up eight'. Don't stay lying down- the moment you fail is the moment you give up, not the moment you fall. A boxer may be able to punch, but their true test lies with how hard they can *get* punched- you can have all the skills, talent, luck, and capital in the world, but if you collapse and quiver with fear after one setback, then you are doomed to live an unfulfilling life.

As a perfectionist, I struggle with this. As you've already read and even now, I create detailed and vivid plans for how I want my near future to unfold. I set a goal that simply must be achieved and outline all the steps that *must* be taken to get there. I know exactly how I want things to go and plan each step in accordance with that vision. Should one of those small steps become jeopardised however, my mentality descends into a panic and I get into an almighty strop. 'It's all ruined!' I may lament, but the cause is only really lost the moment you decide to drop all other steps and give up. Dropping the whole endeavour because one small piece has failed- how pitiful does that sound? Why must the entire project suffer just because one task cannot be completed to perfection?

Perfectionism can spur us onto assessing finer details and ensuring we always produce our best quality. However, perfectionists often fall into the trap of 'analysis paralysis'. By obsessing over perfection, we may well end up producing nothing at all. I know many talented people with infinite levels of creativity who have the potential to produce wonderful things, but I fear they may never accomplish their dreams simply because they feel there are too many reasons at any given time why they cannot produce their finest work. For the perfectionists out there: once we lie on our death beds and reflect on our lives and what we've produced and accomplished, we will derive the most pride and satisfaction from what we *actually* did, right? Allow me to rephrase. Looking back on what you *could've* produced or accomplished instead of what you *actually* accomplished will most likely make you feel regretful, not proud. Therefore it is vital- just as it was for me in the early months of 2017- that upon receiving a setback we learn to rebalance our expectations, re-plan our route to success, reconsider areas that can be further improved, and continue on our quest for the end goal.

For runners, it is important to accept that injuries can and probably will come to haunt us when we least want them to. Injuries will probably occur during training and they might even occur on the week of your event. Sometimes- despite your best measures to prevent an injury- they happen anyway, even if it's not your fault. Unfortunately, that's just life. Many people who have tried running do not accept this, and for this reason their initial ambitions of either becoming healthier, losing weight, or running a marathon all ultimately fail. Notice how all those examples that include different types of goals are grouped together? This lack of acceptance can detriment any goal from the most essential to the most ambitious. Note that this is not just for running either. Refusing to accept setbacks in any venture of your life may lead you to give up on some of your potentially great achievements, and that would be a proper shame that you will almost certainly regret at some point.

As I stared myself down in the mirror on that night in February 2017, I realised I had to continue my efforts even with the injuries that extinguished all the fiery motivation that was responsible for my early strides. I realised I could not rely on the motivation from running to work productively on my university studies. Once running was taken out of the equation, my entire life seemed to collapse- this could not be allowed to continue. I therefore realised that I had to learn to run without running, just like I had to learn to work without running, i.e. make steps towards the end goal even with the actual act of running temporarily unfeasible.

Above all, I had to learn to continue even without the motivation nor with circumstances in my favour. I needed to develop the type of mindset that could circumvent negative thoughts and feelings and just act. Willpower was what I needed.

Reckless excess and The Great Knee Debate

My knee may have been injured from overuse and abuse, but as far as I was aware, the rest of my body functioned fine. Plus, my mind- which was about to free itself from being a slave to my mood- also still functioned. That's the core of willpower: whether your mood is euphoric or rotting in a depression, you and your mind keep working towards the task at hand without question. If there is one thing that never changes, it's that there is no time like the present; *now* was the time to act and creatively continue to prepare for the marathon in May and beyond, even if running wasn't possible for a while. Now was the time to work smarter.

The first step to this required the complete eradication of reckless excess. After all, my problems with injury, fatigue, and motivation all fell into the same category, whereby I ran myself to injury by exerting beyond a level that was sustainable. Reckless excess is the true culprit behind many running injuries, not running itself. Blaming running has become a popular excuse for people's reckless excess, and it has led to the widespread rhetoric that running is 'bad for the knees'. It's a phrase tossed around by people who maintain a negative opinion towards running and mostly originates from their unsuccessful attempts to run, or by listening to someone who once tried running and made a complete hash of it. These kinds of beliefs shift the responsibility away from ourselves and often result in bitter failure.

You can bet that the vast majority of those who say running is bad for your knees have given up on the sport because they injured their own knees at some point- pay close attention to the transitive verb choice. It was not the fault of running itself, nor their bodies as exogenous factors, but their own: they most likely ran *themselves* to injury and then blamed it on the entire sport. These are the very people who give up once the setback of an injury strikes and for that reason, it would be smart not to listen to them. Strikingly however, many people blindingly do.

To clear this up once and for all: running is not bad for your knees, in fact it is actually good for them. This should not be a surprise, because after all it is exercise; you are always better off living a runner's lifestyle as opposed to a sit-around-and-do-nothing-all-day lifestyle. Those that cry running will wreck your knees are referring to the development of osteoarthritis, but the logic is backwards as years of studies prove. Let's briefly touch upon what the scientific research tells us.[6]

For starters, in experiments focusing on knee osteoarthritis, runners always have lower rates than non-runners.[7] In a study that measured the health of runners and non-runners over 20 years, symptoms of arthritis were discovered in 32% of non-runners compared to only 20% for runners.[8] For older runners, the health

---

[6] Research round-up partly sourced from Runner's World, 2020. Will Running Ruin Your Knees? Here Are the Facts.
https://www.runnersworld.com/health-injuries/a32598733/is-running-bad-for-your-knees/

[7] Alentorn-Geli, E., Samuelsson, K., Musahl, V., Green, C. L., Bhandari, M., & Karlsson, J. (2017). The Association of Recreational and Competitive Running With Hip and Knee Osteoarthritis: A Systematic Review and Meta-analysis. *The Journal of orthopaedic and sports physical therapy*, 47(6), 373–390.

[8] Chakravarty EF, Hubert HB, Lingala VB, Zatarain E, Fries JF. Long distance running and knee osteoarthritis. A prospective study. *Am J Prev Med*. 2008;35(2):133-138.

improvements are even more profound; in a study that tracked the physical conditions of 50-year-old participants over 21 years, regular runners had significantly less limitations compared to non-runners, and as a handy bonus, more of them were still alive.[9]

Osteoarthritis was once thought of as a gradual breakdown of the cartilage, henceforth running had been perceived as the long-term detriment to maintaining healthy tissues. However, this interpretation is no longer accepted. Instead, running is now seen as a promoter of healthy cartilage by conditioning it to become more resilient and durable.[10] Osteoarthritis is now believed to be caused by disease to the joint, notably brought about by obesity. As healthy runners have a lower BMI, they mitigate the risk of this disease by placing less weight on their joints when moving compared to someone who is overweight.[11]

Finally, as a final hurrah of evidence before we get lost in academia, running can particularly work to your benefit if your knees are already in poor condition. In a study focussing on middle-aged participants, MRI scans showed that after a four-month marathon training programme, participants' knee cartilage

---

[9] Chakravarty EF, Hubert HB, Lingala VB, Fries JF. (2008) Reduced Disability and Mortality Among Aging Runners: A 21-Year Longitudinal Study. *Arch Intern Med.*;168(15):1638–1646.

[10] Miller RH. Joint Loading in Runners Does Not Initiate Knee Osteoarthritis. *Exerc Sport Sci Rev*. 2017;45(2):87-95.

[11] Williams PT. Effects of running and walking on osteoarthritis and hip replacement risk. *Med Sci Sports Exerc*. 2013;45(7):1292-1297. doi:10.1249/MSS.0b013e3182885f26

was in *better* condition than at the start of the programme[12]- is that not amazing?

Therefore, based upon this real evidence, it should offend you- or at the very least shock you- to hear that people genuinely think running is bad for the knees. As you can imagine, reckless excess gives you some ridiculously muddled opinions alongside a pair of dodgy knees. The reason my knee became injured was not because of running, but because *I* put too much stress on my joints and overdid the mileage. We will therefore round off this little science section with a reminder that you must learn your body's limits to reap running's benefits in full and avoid any nasty reckless excess.

3 ways to improve your running without running

With the great knee debate finally out of the way, I will now share three ways in which I continued my marathon training and improved my physical ability without taking a single step in my running shoes. Just because you're injured and unable to run doesn't mean you can't condition yourself to be stronger and better equipped to safely push yourself once your injuries are healed. These things may seem like common sense, but the more diligently you follow them the greater they will serve you. In fact, to be a complete risk-free runner, putting at least moderate effort into these three is essential.

---

[12] Horga LM, Henckel J, Fotiadou A, et al. Can marathon running improve knee damage of middle-aged adults? A prospective cohort study. BMJ Open Sport & Exercise Medicine 2019;5:e000586. doi:10.1136/bmjsem-2019-000586

First, I became a yogi, which if you told me that a year earlier while I was screaming my lungs out to 'Will Griggs on fire' at 2:30am in a club, I'd probably have sobered up straight away. I never imagined myself foraying onto a yoga mat but three years on it's another choice I'm proper glad I made. Similar to running, yoga offers deep mental and physical relief, not to mention it's a great way to reach a meditative state. As someone who doesn't like to sit still, the movement and full-body-experience of yoga stimulates my mind and helps me to see any situation from a more calm and rational perspective. After each session, there's always a soothing reassurance that things are going to be all right.

There are so many different forms of yoga which can target different areas of your body, stimulate your mind depending on the kind of boost you need, and provide relief and strengthening to injured areas. If there's one resource you need to get started then look no further than the Yoga With Adriene YouTube channel.[13]

Adriene is the internet's queen of yoga, leading over 7 million yogis with her slogan, 'Find what feels good'. She has a huge collection of yoga videos that range from 5 to 10-minute quick routines, to themed routines ranging from 15 to 40 minutes, and longer, full practices at 40 minutes and over. Legs tired after a long run? Try 'Yoga for Tired Legs'. Need a surge in creativity? Try 'Yoga for Artists' or 'Yoga for Writers'. Need a pick-up after a bad day? 'Yoga for When You're In a Bad Mood' is what you want. Whatever the mood, whatever the feeling in your body, Adriene's got you covered. She's a top pal to do yoga alongside; gentle,

---

[13] www.youtube.com/user/yogawithadriene

supporting, and also very funny- no wonder her fans love her to bits- and no, I'm not getting paid to write this![14]

The one sure way to immediately boost your running is through yoga. Knowing that I could be out for a considerable amount of time, I started one of Adriene's 30-day yoga 'journeys' to build up the self-discipline, dedication, and muscle flexibility to ensure I restarted training as a smarter and more capable runner.

Within 10 days I saw results. My flexibility improved tenfold, my ability to manage and regulate my breathing improved, and I also felt able to mentally take a step back from my restrictive situation and cast a positive eye on proceedings, recognising the solid progress I was making. After every session I felt relieved of my troubles and reassured that these setbacks really weren't the end of the world. As Adriene once said, for runners, the relationship with our breath is key; once I eventually did return to running, the ability to consciously manage my breath brought substantial improvements to my stamina and speed. There's no doubt about it- running and yoga are terrific complements. Grab yourself a mat and experience the benefits from your own home.

The next big change was taking greater advantage of my gym membership. While the act of running will make your joints and muscles more durable, strengthening exercises and resistance training in the gym will train your body to be tougher and

---

[14] Although if you're reading this Adriene and would like to do a sponsorship deal then please do email ejameswarren@gmail.com that'd be quality x

stronger, allowing for increased running efficiency (run harder, tire less!), greater speed, and more resilience to injury.

Many injury-prone runners will benefit from building more muscle. It should be noted that there is a difference between owning a body compromising of lean muscle and owning a body which resembles a flimsy twig, snapping and collapsing under high intensity. Those worrying that hitting the gym will bulk them up and raise their weight and BMI ought to remember that higher muscle mass is favourable to flab; you may be heavier but you have the muscle to support your joints when they take stress from the roads.

Gym training doesn't have to be deadlifts, bench press, and arm curls. The most beneficial exercises for runners are squats, lunges, planks, and anything with a resistance band tied around your ankles- the list is enormous, so there's a great variety to the routines you can try which will keep your gym workouts fresh and enjoyable.

A good start would be with this routine from *Runner's World*[15]:
1. Plank- 45-60 seconds (3-5 reps)
2. Russian Twists (10-12 reps)
3. Scorpion (3-5 reps on each leg)
4. Back Extension (10-12 reps)
5. Squat to Overhead Press (10-12 reps)
6. Overhead Forward Lunge (6-8 reps on each leg)
7. Stability Ball Jackknife (10-12 reps)
8. Stability Ball Leg Curl (6-8 reps)
9. Rotational Shoulder Press (6-8 reps)
10. Alternating Row (10-12 reps)

To complete this routine, all you'll need is a mat, a couple of weights, and a stability ball- equipment all available in just about every gym. Or, if you prefer home workouts, purchasing this equipment is relatively cheap and will last you years- yes, this routine can be easily done from your own home or in your garden, so a gym membership isn't required.

To make the routine harder as your body adapts, add in more reps. Always aim to perform each exercise slowly to stimulate your muscles as much as possible- never cheat yourself when it comes to form! This routine will cover all key areas of your legs, tighten your core, and tone your muscles. Completing it twice a week will have huge benefits on your physical health and running. If it all seems quite a lot, then perhaps start by doing the first five exercises on one day and the latter five on the other. Once again, gradual

---

[15] www.runnersworld.com/training/a20805692/10-essential-strength-exercises-for-runners/

and progressive intensity is key here- let's not delve into any reckless excess.

The third change was nutrition. Admittedly, once injury struck, my cooking habits reverted back to term 1 standards. Slipping into lazy cooking habits acted as blatant proof that I lacked the self-discipline required not just for running, but to survive as a functional adult. As I set about getting my cooking back on track, I learnt about the type of meals that would suit my budget-constrained lifestyle. I learnt I needed to up my protein intake drastically to recover from the increased stress loads, and to fuel my muscles with the energy needed to tackle each session required lots more carbohydrates.

When it comes to cooking, I won't go into any fancy details about the recipes and macros and whatnot- there are plenty of great runner's cookbooks out there which will cover the subject much better than I could ever hope to.[16] Instead, I will mention cooking as an important area to consider because it formed the basis for creating willpower while I was injured, just like the other two changes mentioned above.

To cook a healthy meal requires far more effort- and far more self-discipline- than simply chucking a ready meal in the microwave. Henceforth, by getting into the habit of cooking healthily even when you really didn't feel motivated, you consolidate good habits.

All three of these elements are important to consider, because despite being different, each of them developed the same strength:

---

[16] *The Runner's Cookbook* by Anita Bean is my personal favourite.

willpower. Yes, yoga improves your flexibility and is wonderfully relaxing, the gym strengthens your muscles and prepares you to run faster and more efficiently, and the cooking improves your overall health, aids recovery, and tops up your energy levels. Those are all additional benefits derived from developing the willpower to do them in the first place. Even without running, by pursuing these three elements you can take huge strides towards becoming more healthy, active, and autonomous.

Because believe me, there were many days when I couldn't be bothered to stretch on the yoga mat, or head to the gym, or cook three decent meals for myself. I would tell myself that I was too busy with more pressing matters; essays had to be written and presentations had to be practised- there was always a reason for not doing them. I eventually accepted that they were all excuses, and that saying you're too busy is actually just the most common form of laziness. The reality is, we've always got something going on in our lives. 'Busy' is just another word for procrastinating. If you're busy now, then you'll always be too busy, won't you? You'll never get anything done.

The truth is, if you really care about something then you will find the time for it. I knew that I really wanted to run this marathon, so I finally promised myself that I would never, ever, be too busy to work on the fundamentals of keeping fit and healthy, even if my 'superpower' of running was temporarily stripped from me. Even if I *didn't* want to master the fundamentals, and even if I felt that burning desire to run the marathon in May begin to fade, I had signed up and made a commitment to myself. I promised myself I would become better because this goal was tied to university, which I wanted to turn into a positive experience. I signed up because I didn't want to be depressed and I wanted to be better. Therefore, no questions asked, no excuses made, I would perform every task the best I could regardless of whether I was motivated or not- such is the influence of willpower.

Blessed by a miracle

Following this realisation, I had finally freed myself from my abusive relationship with motivation. No longer did I need it. No longer would it dictate my actions. Thanks to willpower, I could do anything regardless of what my mood told me to do. My knee injury demoralised me considerably, just like the ankle injury before; I wondered if I could ever train for my marathon without getting injured every week, I wondered if running a marathon was even possible for me. These two injuries revealed severe weaknesses in my character, but breakdowns lead to breakthroughs. Thanks to the limitations of injury I was able to research and implement these three elements to improve my running and overall health, and also develop the willpower that would spur me onto continued and stable progress once I could run again.

I felt as if I had overcome a significant personal trial, overseen and judged by the three sages: yoga, the gym, and nutrition. After cementing these three elements into my routine, I became able to confidently say to myself that I would diligently continue them for the benefit of my mental and physical health, regardless of whether or not I could ever run again. Sounds dramatic I know, but the important message remains: You should never tie your wellbeing entirely to running, otherwise injuries will sink you to dangerous and terribly unproductive lows. Running should be an enhancer of your life like a committed partnership, but not to the point where you lose your identity- sounds like a romantic relationship, doesn't it? We can't rely on our partners for happiness and success because at the end of the day that comes from ourselves. Rather, by being supportive characters for each other, we're encouraged to get the best out of ourselves. I believe that my eventual understanding of this concept prepared me for a triumphant and almost magical return to running.

What if I told you I found the most amazing remedy for runner's knee? What if I told you it allowed me to resume running almost straight away, with pain at a minimum? After weeks of angst and agony, I discovered the missing piece required to solve this injury puzzle. Runner's knee, for all the horror and grief it gave me, has a very effective remedy. And no, it's nothing dodgy or illegal and it doesn't involve strange herbal medicines that you have to buy through the dark web using Bitcoin. It's not a secret, but it's not as well-known as it probably should be.

The magical instrument was- wait for it- an ingeniously simple brace known as a 'patella strap'. It's a small Velcro strap that fits around the front of your knee and holds it comfortably in place during movement so that the patella doesn't cause any friction against the cartilage, preventing irritation of inflamed areas. Not to be confused with an IT band strap, which is for injuries on the outer area of your knee.

When I first set out with the strap, I was unsurprisingly very nervous, remembering all the previous failed attempts to run that were merely met by more stiff pain. This time however, there was nothing- it was remarkable. My pain was completely absent, and it felt like my knee was recovering while I could still run. Even though there was a slight ache in the injured area towards the end of the run, in the future sessions that ache gradually disappeared until I could run at any intensity without any knee pain at all. As a precaution, I opted to keep it on for the rest of training.

And so, the marathon dream was alive once more. This time with yoga routines, gym workouts, and a healthier nutrition strategy – now we were ready to make moves! Injury ordeals like this really do reinforce a sense of gratitude that we can simply run without struggle and repositions the importance of running in our lives. Thanks to this experience, running became a fond friend, rather than a toxic partner where you're guilty of chronic attachment issues.

Looking back on the entire injury experience also made me recognise the considerable changes in mindset. Running had a different place in my life; it was now just one aspect in which I could work on self-development, but out of everything I've ever tried, nothing teaches you more about yourself than running. It opens doors for other avenues to explore which ensures your physical and mental health remain in top condition. You can diversify your interests, meaning that should one become jeopardised then you still have the others to enjoy.

I felt so grateful for this personal journey of discovery- it had certainly not gone the way I anticipated but that was the beauty of it. I initially imagined a straightforward rising path of improvement, when in actual fact, the journey is full of highs and lows (pardon the cliché). Eventually, you realise that if you can learn your lessons, then each low serves to catapult you to greater highs- that is the real nature of progress.

Direct or indirect, running was indeed changing my life. As such, once I settled into marathon training, I took the opportunity to give back a little while taking the next big step. I decided that on the week I was due to run half marathon distance for my long run, I would enter the Silverstone Half Marathon- the first taste of a real, large-scale running event. To make the occasion even more special, I decided to run it in support of a small children's charity and launch a fundraiser.

As the next two chapters chronicle, this event became one of the most cherished memories in my entire running journey. And hereafter, we enjoy the wonderful merits of being a smart runner.

Make sure you learn your lessons, because now the real adventure can begin.

Part Three: Merits

Chapter 8
How to run for charity and why you'll love it

Running for a charity could well be the most rewarding experience out of your entire running adventure. It can expand your personal quest into something which will make a valuable contribution to those in need.

Fundraising for charity is remarkably popular in the running community. Just one look at the field of the London Marathon each year and you'll witness a sea of colour- that'll be the vests of charity runners donning the name and colours of their cause. In fact, any event you see will be awash with ordinary people doing extraordinary things for the noblest of reasons. We may call these people ordinary, but the truth is each and every one of them are extraordinary and inspirational heroes in their own unique ways.

In 2019, the London Marathon raised over £66,400,000 for hundreds of charities, smashing its own world record for an annual single-day charity fundraising event for the thirteenth year in a row. Since the inaugural event in 1981, the London Marathon has raised over £1 billion (that's £1,000,000,000!).

By simply tuning into the broadcast of one of the world's most famous marathons you will likely get inspired by the moving stories of all the individuals who make up the 50,000-strong field. To think that in such great numbers comes so many profound personal battles is mind-blowing but consider this: the London Marathon makes up just one event in the whole running calendar. Across the country and the entire world there are events, organisations, and individuals raising money, support, and awareness for important causes.

When deciding to enter a running event, participating with a charity is of course completely optional. But there are so many reasons why it will enhance your experience tenfold. Running for a charity will empower you with a team willing you on each step of the way; it will add a new dimension to your running journey and of course, it will have a positive impact on those in which your campaign aims to help.

When I mention you'll gain a team, I mean this in two ways. Firstly, your cause will delight and inspire your close network around you; friends and family will marvel at your compassionate decision. Whether it's through words of encouragement or even a monetary contribution, the support of your friends and family will add an extra spring in your step to every training session, giving you even more great reasons to get out of bed in the morning and go for a run.

Secondly, you'll have the actual charity supporting you as well. This is why fundraising is such a joy because every charity I've ever worked with have always gone the extra mile to ensure I have the best experience with them. We'll cover the thrills of working with charities in its own section.

With these support networks in mind, I will base this chapter on the story of my first fundraiser and how it helped me reach out beyond my close networks, connecting me with my classmates and wider community at university.

Selecting a cause

The first step in evolving your personal journey into something that also inspires and supports others is selecting your cause and finding a charity to run for. Luckily, a lot of big events offer the option to sign up for a charity during registration- this is how I originally started my campaign. When I signed up for the 2017 Silverstone Half Marathon, I decided upon Rainbow Trust, a small charity that provides emotional and practical support to families who have a child with a life-threatening or terminal illness.[17]

While I had no personal experience of the cause behind Rainbow Trust's endeavours, a look through their website, their stories, and their people quickly drew me in- I saw the hard work of the staff and the parents in caring for their children and felt a

---

[17] www.rainbowtrust.org.uk – Do give them a visit- they're a wonderful organisation run by wonderful people.

strong empathy and resonation; it made me think that if I were to ever have a child, then whatever the circumstances, my support for them would be unconditional. Therefore, seeing the families and the charity put in such hard work really spoke to me and so it was thus my pleasure to represent the organisation.

In addition, after reading about their fundraising events, I realised that even though they are a smaller charity, they put in a tremendous effort to help their runners have an enjoyable fundraising experience. Their people were as bright and bubbly as their organisation's logo and colours, and I increasingly felt a strong will to support them just as I believe they harboured a strong will to support me.

Upon confirming Rainbow Trust as my charity option for Silverstone, I received an email thanking me for choosing them and offering the first steps in setting up a fundraiser. I hopped over to Virgin Money Giving[18] to create my own unique page where I could add updates, photos, videos, and track the total amount of donations raised.

As my fundraiser began to take shape, I found myself thoroughly enjoying keeping my page as informative, personal, and stylised as can be. By linking Rainbow Trust's site and media to the page, potential donors could see the cause behind my half marathon attempt, while posting updates gave supporters a check-in on how training and preparation was going. I felt like I was at the helm of a real positive movement. Managing my own

---

[18] www.uk.virginmoneygiving.com – A great site for hosting your own fundraiser. Alternative platforms include GoFundMe and JustGiving.

fundraiser was highly rewarding, not to mention convenient. By having your own fundraising webpage, you have a centralised link to all your activities, easily shareable with anyone you meet.

Receiving cool goodies

One of the great things about running for charity is undoubtedly the sense of belonging and community when joining a charity's 'team'. Once you're signed up, most charities make sure you're kitted out and well equipped to smash your fundraising campaign.

Most charities offer you a neat little fundraising pack for free if you request one from their website. With Rainbow Trust, I received one as soon as I registered for Silverstone. A standard for most charities is to supply their runners with the charity's official running vest, which on most occasions you receive for free.

With Rainbow Trust I received a beautifully designed vest which had a white base with the colours of the rainbow immaculately printed over the chest and the crisp and clean font of the Rainbow Trust logo on the front- it's the one I'm wearing on the cover of this book!

I felt a genuine sense of pride wearing it, because having the uniform and embodying the organisation evoked feelings of belonging. While I had never met the staff nor my fellow fundraising runners, it felt as if we were together and united in our cause. Considering my university life up to that point had been largely a solitary experience where I felt alienated from my school and community, feeling even a flicker of attachment from the charity was warming.

Also included in the fundraising pack was a card net to cut, fold, and assemble into a little donations box. Alongside that, there was a very amusing afro hat in rainbow colours which, if I hadn't been battling crippling self-esteem issues back then, would've probably loved wearing. The effort these charities put into creating fun little fundraising packs is admirable and thanks to this initiative, runners have an easy point of access into creating their own campaigns.

For bigger charities at bigger events, you may even get a large tent area set up by the organisations themselves, dedicated to their runners in the event paddock. Inside you can meet staff and other runners, receive running gels and energy drinks- not to mention chocolate and sweets of course- and maybe even get a massage.

Even for smaller charities, there will be a tent in which you can meet the staff and just relax and soak up the race day atmosphere. Again, the emphasis here is that you'll feel part of a larger collective; you will be welcomed with open arms into a family and given unbounded support in return for your dedication during your fundraising activities. It's a wonderfully beneficial relationship. For those that aren't too keen on joining official running clubs, or who may still be looking for a solid, concrete reason that will ignite their passion for running, finding and joining a charity which works for a cause you can sympathise with and support may drive you a long way.

Fundraising

How does one go about fundraising? I see it as a question of creativity. The most effective fundraising ideas don't require large capital- they're usually just fun and creative. The first important thing to make sure of is your fundraiser's reachability. Is the website set up and looking pristine? Are the instructions on how to donate clear? These are the fundamentals that are handy to have checked off before you begin. Trust me, I spent many afternoons during my campaign messaging friends and family back and forth helping them navigate the donation pages. The quicker and easier it is for donors to give money the more likely people will go through with the contribution- this means decluttering the multiple links and webpages if and where possible.

Next, think of ideas on how you can spread the word. Writing posts on your social media accounts is the easiest way to introduce your campaign and offer updates, just make sure the link to your fundraising page is consistently visible- the link is the key to finding donors! Put it into your Instagram and Twitter bio, position it on the top line of every post, and even add it to your email signature- without the link donors cannot contribute.

Going a step beyond the simple social media post, you can write blog articles and create cool posters to build a sense of anticipation for your big event. At the beginning of 2017, I started a blog to document my university life; once running became a more significant factor in my daily ongoings, I stepped up my running coverage and began documenting the journey on a weekly basis. Once the charity campaign got underway, this became my main communication point with my supporters who were eager to see how training was going.[19]

Making posters is a particularly fun way to spread awareness for your campaign. Obviously the option to hand draw and photocopy posters detailing your mission and charity details is there, but for me I got a great kick out of editing a photo of me in my running gear on GIMP and adding the donation links and charity logo which I could use to spread around my social media.

We're getting steadily more creative, so let's introduce some more fun ideas. Fundraising doesn't have to be a marketing exercise, instead, you can put your baking skills to the test by preparing a batch of cupcakes to sell at school or work. Selling homemade creations is definitely one of the most enjoyable ways to fundraise. Granted, if you're naff at baking like me then you might have a horrific afternoon ahead of you, spiralling into full blown disaster when you realise you've overdone the sugar and all your customers are uncontrollably projectile vomiting all around you.[20] If you're competent in the kitchen then this'll be a blast. And what's more, you can regard earning donations as no longer like a pure sale, but rather like a trade; customers will happily buy a nice cupcake off you regardless of whether they are fully engaged with your charity work.

---

[19] It's also worth noting that writing a blog is highly rewarding in the long run, providing a personal time machine to chronicle the lessons and memories of your past adventures- I still read back on old posts today and re-absorb their wisdom.

[20] This didn't actually happen, by the way. Okay, maybe once.

If, like me, you tend to be shy when approaching people, then a flashy display of goodies will bring people to you. Finally, if baking really isn't your forte, then the most straightforward option by far is to just buy a big box of Dunkin Donuts and sell those individually, it'll save you an afternoon and a potential home insurance claim if it all kicks off in the oven.

Staying on the subject of food, you can invite all your mates around one evening for a pot-luck style feast of all different types of meals, maybe even basing it on a particular theme such as international cuisine. Buffets are another good option, where similarly you can charge a small admission fee before letting your guests run riot. Alternatively, you could invite a sizeable group of friends and family out to a restaurant and negotiate with the owner whether a percentage of the bill can go towards your charity. Other ideas include hosting a raffle where you sell tickets for a grand prize, and car boot sales- both of which are a great way of decluttering unused items clogging up storage space, turning them into funds which will go a long way for your fundraiser. Don't be afraid to pounce on unique opportunities that may come your way either- not only were my university lecturers happy to let me address the class in between breaks, but I also got to do a short speech about my fundraiser in my university's bar and received a nice shoutout in the student union's newsletter.

Whichever of these ideas you decide to try, they are all undoubtedly great opportunities to take a break from the fast-paced working lifestyles we lead and spend some quality time connecting and sharing experiences with those important to us, or those we're yet to get to know properly. Running for charity is a shared adventure, a collective joy. By involving as many good people around you as possible, it's sure to become one of the highlights of your year. For me, my fundraiser was at the forefront of the week in which my university life finally hit its stride. Thanks to the positivity I was able to spread through running, I at long last broke the deadlock and made friends with my classmates.

Embraced by everyone's encouragement

Up until now, my running journey had been entirely private and personal. Even during the great highs of my early running experiences, I kept everything to myself and wasn't at all fussed about showing the world my progress. When the injuries came, and everything went tits up, you bet I felt glad of that decision. But, once lessons had finally been learned and my daily routine eventually stabilised, the idea to run for charity gave me an avenue to share what I had decided to dedicate myself towards.

Furthermore, and this may strike you as odd, it gave me a topic that would add value and contribute- something to actually talk about in those small and awkward conversations before class. Up until now, I had been unchanged in my relationship with my university campus since chapter 1. But this was where it changed. Now I had something to talk about. Now I had something to be passionate about and connect with others. No longer would I be a passive listener with nothing to say amidst this wave of characters in the melting pot that is London- finally, I had an identity.

The week of 6th-12th March 2017 was one of the most magical seven days of my life. It was to be an immensely busy week: two presentations in my Japanese culture lecture and developmental economics tutorial, followed by a mid-term exam in my Japanese class, a whole 2,500-word economics essay, all before finally climaxing with the big one- the Silverstone Half Marathon. Having made the necessary changes to avoid burnout and having gradually developed my self-discipline and willpower over the past few weeks, I knew that I had prepared enough to make this week an overwhelming whopper of success. This was where running (with a great debt also to the charity campaign) truly began to influence other areas.

In the fortnight prior, I grappled with the task of two presentations and three essays in just four weeks, a workload I had not yet experienced prior to entering university. During the injury phase, the prospect terrified me but having overcome the setbacks with these new tools for success I learnt how to break each task down to match realistic expectations. With the mammoth task ahead, I bolstered my productivity through accepting that these essays wouldn't write themselves and that with clever planning, the right level of dedication, and smart exertion of effort, I could complete each and every single task to the best of my ability and earn the top grades.

I would do this by dedicating three days to research at the beginning of the week, followed by writing the essay section by section, and then finishing the assignment no matter how long it took on Sunday. I also planned to review and redraft a week later, so I could look back on my work with fresh eyes.

This was doable. Confidence and self-belief were blossoming. I owe this to the lessons learnt from running; it instils in you a steeliness that does not squirm at the prospect of injuries nor big piles of assignments. Rather, it encourages you to break each task down and steadily chip away. Then, thanks to willpower, not only can you plan for success, but effectively execute that plan, too.

By sticking to my plans I fully saw the significance of each daily task and learnt to be mindful of the present; no longer would I daydream or wonder in angst about the outcomes of the future as the time to work on them was now.

This inspired unprecedented levels of dedication into my work. When creating my first economics presentation, a 20-minute analysis on the history of India's economic development, I let my perfectionism run wild and strived for a detailed and professional PowerPoint slideshow. As such, slide information was immaculately laid out, each figure correctly sized, cropped, outlined, and referenced, each graph labelled for ease of viewing, and every slide neatly ordered into an easy to follow structure. My essays followed a similar fashion. Each assignment was researched to construct at least a three-page bibliography, sorted into a table of contents that outlined the main arguments of every topic, and formatted and proofread to the point of no errors or inconsistencies at all. I had never taken so much pride in my work. By the end of each week I would have a completed presentation or essay that I would feel proud and even excited to submit.

My presentations received extra special attention. Despite considering myself the shy introverted type I love presenting in front of an audience things I've worked hard on. I spent hours preparing my presentations to the point where I could recite all twenty minutes off by heart- first memorising the script, then being able to run through it without errors, and then finally being able to perform it. Why did I go through all this effort? Because I finally understood and believed that if you put the hard work in then sky's the limit- talent and natural ability don't matter when you can guide pure hard work in a focused direction.

Once the busiest week of all came around, the lessons and efforts of the past few months finally started to show results. First of all, the economics presentation went like a dream. When the big day came around there were no nerves, just pure excitement for what I was about to perform. I dressed nicely (coincidentally wearing matching colours to my PowerPoint presentation's theme) and addressed the room full of familiar strangers with a big smile. All 20 minutes went to perfection. The lecturer- who was quite an intense and critical type- loved it, commended my efforts, and awarded the highest grade in the class.

However, what followed after class was for me the most memorable part. So many of my classmates whom I've never shared a word with came up to congratulate me on my presentation. Having suddenly been thrust into the limelight, pre-running Ellis would've probably shrugged off the compliments and never followed up. Fortunately, once we all became engaged in a conversation that transcended economics work, I was able to stand my ground for once. Perhaps you'll laugh upon reading that phrasing, but as an anxious teenager it was a huge victory! Not only was I able to talk about my running but could give a concrete example of my ambitions by mentioning the half marathon and the charity campaign. As I told my tales the others quickly picked up on the energy I radiated when speaking. I was told, 'You seem so happy!' and, 'Wow you've really got your life together,' which at first completely took me by surprise. Having gone through the first term of university so unhappy, so chaotically disorganised, and so- well, let's be frank- lonely, I fully realised that I now embodied the very opposite. I realised for the first time in goodness knows how long that I was passionate about something and boy, does passion take you places.

The charity campaign also helped establish a narrative that others could follow. My new friends were eager to read my blog, visit the fundraising website, and of course hear about the big event on Sunday. To have people who cared about something I felt passionate towards meant so much back then. For the first time I believed I was beginning to finally make meaningful connections at university. It didn't require anything to change but myself. By following my passion as part of a road towards a better me, it attracted good people with similar ambitions. The emphasis here is that running doesn't just attract runners as friends, but in my experience, it attracts people who just like you, are looking to make positive changes in their life, who are striving towards a goal, and approach each day with a purpose. Whichever way you look at it, we need people like that in our lives. They're great supporters and without realising, a mirror for us to gauge whether we are performing at our best.

The second presentation that week blessed me with similar results. Having shown the more driven and confident version of myself to the class, I was now making friends with classmates from both of my departments and all of a sudden, had a small following as the day in which I set foot around Silverstone drew nearer. All that stood ahead was the mid-term Japanese exam and this week's essay, but both were completed with the same care and pride in good time, the latter of which was completed after an 'all-dayer', which consisted of sitting indoors with the curtains closed for the entire day, writing until the essay was submission ready.

As I approached the night before the half marathon, I wrote a brief blog acknowledging that life felt simply amazing at that very point in time. Here's a quote from that particular post that summed up my delight in making new friends:

> '[My university] is starting to feel a lot smaller now, in the sense that I'm finally starting to recognise a community, despite being in four completely different classes. I feel like I'm rediscovering myself again, and lately each day has felt a lot more rewarding. On Friday, Paul let me join him, Victor, and Tommy for one of their weekly basketball sessions. I can honestly say I had a blast and didn't expect to enjoy basketball so much. I find myself looking ahead in excitement now for the next week.'[21]

---

[21] https://elliswarrensite.wordpress.com/2017/03/12/flying/

I was flying. I could sense myself gradually finding my place in the university's social sphere, running was going well, and the charity campaign had started to really gain traction.

Taking my running journey public was not something I planned to do in January but given the situation now I was sure glad I did. I now had a team of family and friends from inside university and out. Support surrounded and empowered me. I felt grateful, because everyone who knew about my big goal genuinely wanted me to reach it. And overall, whether people could understand my deeper reasons for wanting to run or not, the charity campaign was a great addition to the journey because of how easy it was for people to get onboard. Thanks to the campaign, my running journey became a shared experience, all while raising money for families supporting ill children.

This chapter has looked at the reasons why charity running can be so fulfilling and told of how it helped me reach out for support from family and friends, both old and new. If you ever you need a good reason to commit to an event you've been wondering about, then working with a charity is a great way to go about it. It keeps you accountable to your goals and the support is always fantastic, whether it be from your closer network or from the charity itself- when you support others, they genuinely will support you back.

I had a blast organising my fundraiser; it amplified my excitement for my first ever running event tenfold. The reason for this was that I've never felt more supported and appreciated by my friends and family before- they made me feel like a hero- which I knew I definitely wasn't- I was simply a man with a goal.

That's the thing though, by taking on a personal challenge such as a marathon or a half marathon, you set out to improve yourself; along the way however, that journey can also help others through charity, and before you know it, you become a little bit of a hero in the process. It's no wonder the London Marathon breaks fundraising records year in year out- the field is filled not with ordinary people, but instead extraordinary people doing extraordinary things. Each and every single one of them is a hero, and you could be too.

Chapter 9
The first event:
An unforgettable experience

It's been quite a profound two months, hasn't it? Inspiration, delusion, injury, maturation, revelation... Running had proved a rocky ride, but undoubtably thrilling. I had learnt a tonne about myself through the trials and tribulations of injury and having come out of it more resolute than ever, was ready to put everything I had learnt to the test.

The Adidas Silverstone Half Marathon would be my first ever mass-participant running event. I would line up alongside 10,000 other runners and complete 13.1 miles around the famous Grand Prix circuit, all while completing my fundraiser for Rainbow Trust. Excitement awaited.

Like the night before Christmas

Words cannot describe how excited I was the night before the event. I had just finished another long essay and was free from academic commitments for the next 24 hours. To follow a running cliché, I cooked an entire bag full of pasta and prepared myself to consume all of it in a hefty carb-loading session. I had a slight issue though- finishing the essay late meant I only got around to eating my dinner at about 9pm- not ideal for when you need an early night ahead of an early start the next morning.

Pressed for time, I began shovelling huge ladle-fulls of pasta down my gob, eager to finish the whole bag before bed. While doing so I laid out my kit and attached my unique number from the pre-race pack to my vest. I neatly organised my running tights, pre-race bananas, straps and tape for potential injury, and my shoes with the timing chip attached. Simply seeing all my gear prepared for tomorrow sent the adrenaline pumping. It was a marvellous sight to behold- as if I were readying for battle!

Unfortunately, all this bending down to organise my kit mid-dinner wreaked havoc on my digestion. Suddenly, a tirade of angry little pastas wanted to break free from my throat, causing me to sit down and reconsider that remaining half-kilo waiting to be eaten. Carb-loading is best done more gently, spread across the entire race week. Cramming everything down in one go the night before therefore wasn't the wisest move. I should have been more aware of the time. I certainly wouldn't be able to digest it all before bed and faced the prospect of chundering all over the start line. For that reason, my night's sleep wasn't so comfortable. Part of me was on the verge of bursting with excitement, another part was on the verge of bursting with pasta.

Once light broke on a cloudy and rainy March morning, the pasta remained dormant in my stomach. I awoke with a horrible, sickly sensation spanning from my throat to my gut, reminiscent of the awful splurge of guilt that sits in your innards after a heavy night out drinking. What's more, my right calf felt tight when I tried to walk. What was this? Had I pulled a muscle? I felt very intensely tuned in to every tiny sensation in my body- nothing quite felt how it should. Precautionary measures were thus taken without hesitation- I strapped my whole right calf up in tape and tightened the patella strap around my knee- it was too late to worry about injuries at this point!

I know now that pre-race nerves manifest themselves in many different forms. When thinking of the 13.1 mile run ahead of me, I felt no fear and no anxiety, only the purest buzz of excitement. However, my body interpreted the situation differently. This is of course a reminder of one of our previous lessons in which the mind and the body react in different ways. On this occasion, my body was not injured, but just a bit nervous; it communicated those nerves through slight aches and tightness.

Once Dad pulled up outside the halls, I grabbed my drawstring race bag and set off with my old man to Silverstone. It would be our third visit to the home of British motorsport- the first two were Formula 1 races. If you had told me when I was younger that by the third visit I would be the one on track, it would have been a great boost of confidence to my failing karting career. Except I wasn't there to race in any sense of the word. I *would* be on track, albeit *running* around it- funny how things turn out, isn't it?

The pre-race buzz

'THE NORTH', grimly stated the motorway signs. London may have been a soggy and sorry sight, but Silverstone appeared completely devoid of colour. Twas a cold morning indeed. When we arrived at the carpark only a few vehicles were present. A muted atmosphere settled below the dense and ever darkening clouds. For a brief moment I doubted whether we were in the right place, or if the event was even meant to take place today. No doubt Dad too was puzzled. Then, right on cue, a middle-aged man in remarkably tight leggings stepped out of his car in front of us. Yep, we had come to the right place.

'My man!' I thought to myself, fully prepared to strut out in my own pair of skin-tight leggings and compliment him on the fetching attire. Buoyant with relief, Dad and I headed out of the carpark towards the event paddock. It would be a fairly long and chilly trek around the circuit's outskirts, but the further we walked the more we were joined by a legion of other runners. Most donned a thick coat to ward off the chills while some were wrapped up to the point of suffocation in what looked like recycling bin bags. Whatever keeps you warm, I suppose.

What startled me the most was a considerable number of runners *already running* on their way to the event paddock. Some of whom were even completing laps around the event village. Dad and I were bemused. 'Can't you wait a little longer?' I thought, 'You'll be running 13.1 miles in a hour anyway…' Alas, for them it was their warm up and a legitimate one at that, but I couldn't help but feel a tad confused at the blokes gunning for glory past everyone before the starting gun itself had even gone. It might have looked good at the time, but I figured they'd look like right plonkers if they gassed out during the race.

Once we reached the paddock the atmosphere containing thousands of excited runners gave no care to the rain. Music blared from the speakers; all tunes were requested via Twitter, and I thank whoever it was that suggested 'Come on Eileen'. I thought it a bit disappointing, however unsurprising, that 'Love Machine' by my beloved Morning Musume didn't get considered.

Around the huge paddock area were groups of friends and families excitably chattering away, many runners dressed in bright and florescent colours, some in fancy dress. The more serious cohort packed their gels, taped their legs, and splattered non-chaffing cream all over their tits. Usually this kind of atmosphere would feel intimidating, but not today. This event- like all running events- would not be judged by how I compared to others, for no one else came into the equation. The only competition here was with myself. Multiply that by 10,000, and in about 3-4 hours' time we had the potential for 10,000 winners all going home happy.

For a while, Dad and I soaked up the carnival atmosphere where I did some important warm up stretches and even more crucially, made multiple visits to the toilet. Soon, I caught sight of Rainbow Trust's bright and happy colours and visited their tent.

Inside were all their lovely staff who thanked me for my fundraising efforts and wished me well on the run.

To be honest, at the time I felt a bit embarrassed about mentioning that I had raised what I thought was *only* £350, but I realised soon after that that was the completely wrong way to look at it. It's easy to be blinded by the sensational charity fundraisers that raise hundreds of thousands, even millions[22], but the fact you galvanised the support of your friends, family, and even beyond your close network to raise *any* amount of money shows you had the strong enough initiative to take action and make a difference. The 'go hard or go home' ideology is redundant here; you made a legitimate and helpful contribution, which is *always* better than nothing. I mean, think of the difference you can make to just one family and then imagine if that were you. All of your hard work matters. Charities are always grateful for any contribution you make, whether it be monetary or even just wearing their vest and promoting the cause. With this mutual sense of gratitude, I harboured a warm, excited feeling ahead of the cold and wet two hours that lie ahead.

---

[22] With these internet viral fundraisers, you must be aware that while their endeavours may indeed be extreme and worthy of such attention, all around the world many are taking on similar challenges. Not all get the viral-sensation attention. Just like the video of that kid yodelling in the middle of Walmart, sometimes your sudden fame is determined by the luck of the right person sharing at the right time. My advice is to set out to do something that is personal to you, not personal to the internet.

Soon, the time finally arrived for us runners to head towards our individual start gates. I told Dad to keep warm and look out for me in around a couple of hours' time. Then, I headed off to my first half marathon, brimming with excitement, gracious with gratitude, and most importantly, warmed up to run 13.1 miles. As a marshal pulled the gate open, I hadn't felt adrenaline of this kind rush through my veins in such a very long time. I had my swagger back- my confidence had returned, and my self-esteem was higher than ever before. I knew I was prepared for this. I was ready. All the training up until now, all the injuries, all the doubts and fears- I was ahead of them and they were behind me. Now just fire that gun and watch me smash it!

Cautious opening miles

I may have been raring to go, but little did I know that the start procedure in these huge events is one massive faff. Not to say it's poorly organised- quite the opposite- they just take quite a while. The other 10,000 runners and I waited for around 45 minutes before we eventually began to shuffle towards the start line; by then most of us had already noticed certain troubles.

Waiting in the wet while an icy wind frequently passed through completely reversed the effects of my stretching earlier. Before long, my muscles got bored and stiffened. I tried to counteract the situation by jumping a few times with a few high knees- now those blokes running up and down the pit straight didn't seem so silly after all. Due to the jumping around, my bladder activated once more, but it was too late to turn back and head to the loo at this point.

'I need a wee,' one runner murmured from behind.

For some reason I felt the need to turn around and quip, 'I've already been three times!', as if I were some sort of veteran of the toilet; that was a more dignified way of saying, 'I should've worn a bloody nappy for today.'

Then, at long last, we began the awkward shuffle towards the line. A gigantic pack of runners slowly edged towards the half marathon's official start point. What are you meant to do in these situations? We moved too slowly to run but slightly too quickly to walk. All around me were people ambitiously breaking into running strides, only to then give up when it was apparent that we wouldn't be moving any quicker. I'm sure everyone feels a bit like a knob in these scenarios; if you try to run you look like a muppet but if you walk then you look inferior, like you haven't even bothered training for two months prior. Obviously, we don't care about what others think, so I walked the distance until my timing chip passed over the start line- I could do with conserving the energy anyway.

As the huge start line comes into sight, the crowds grow in numbers and noise, the music thumps against your chest, and the pack gathers pace. Everything speeds up and the adrenaline hits you once more. You edge closer and closer to the start, hit the timing pad, and then you're off! No turning back now. You are now running a half-marathon.

I savoured the moment. This was the *true* beginning of my running journey, full of the glitz and glamour of a Formula 1 circuit, surrounded by thousands of other runners. All the previous injury bollocks was now a thing of the past- my mind was set purely on the next 13.1 miles ahead.

And savour the moment I did. I embarked on my adventure at a snail's pace. Perhaps too much savouring? No, you can never start your first event too slowly. Although mind you, this was a bit on the slow side perhaps even for walking speed. Eager to not join the nutters galloping away like their bladders depended on it, I kept a steady speed to gradually warm my muscles up into the running rhythm. After all, it was a [half] marathon, not a sprint.

Five minutes later and I did start to ask myself, 'is this a bit too slow?' as the *entire* field overtook me. I was going backwards. Even the old nans and grandads were powering past. But this was all part of the test. They could run their own race. Their pace is their responsibility, so I hoped they were ready to maintain it until the end. As for me, I had to respect all 13.1 miles. Start too quick now and I may conk at the end, or worse, pull a muscle at the start. Knowing how injuries had been the bane of my life for much of this journey so far, I knew I'd be better safe than sorry.

As we turned a corner, marshals jumped up and down cheering us on. Music blared from both sides of the track alongside the roar of packed grandstands. It was fully worth starting slow to drink it all in. To think I once wanted to go through the hassle of sponsorships and working my way up the ranks as a racing driver to experience this kind of atmosphere! It was beautiful. With a grin I realised what a stroke of fortune it was to discover this incredible world of running.

I continued with a smile, feeling my heartrate gradually climb but also my bladder impatiently throb. Oh yeah- I proper needed the toilet. One marshal was in possession of a huge bell and rung it so vigorously you'd think the four Kings and Queens of Narnia were about to arrive. I initially mistook it as an indicator that we had already completed the first mile. Without a watch on and no mile signs in sight, I wanted to believe it, but then she shouted, 'You've almost done half a mile!', and I realised the exact distance in which my bladder would have to endure.

Then, when we negotiated the Maggots, Becketts, and Chapel corner complex I witnessed a truly astonishing sight at this world-renowned spot. In 2015, under slippery wet conditions I watched Formula 1 cars spectacularly spin off at this high-speed section, now, two years later, I watched a herd of middle-aged men dart off the circuit towards the tyre barriers desperate for a wee. Turns out the marshal wasn't holding the only bell that needed ringing. Right before my eyes, dozens of blokes lined the Armco, all relieving themselves, separated by a then social distance of about a few feet.

I was half stunned, but half tempted to join them for I was also bursting at this point. I knew I shouldn't. It would be an awful thing to do- Silverstone is the birthplace of British motor racing, full of history, full of pride and memories. It's one of the most internationally and historically renowned racetracks in the world and I was about to wee on it.

A tiny angelic Ellis appeared on my right shoulder and urged me not to do it, but then a demonic Ellis appeared to my left and questioned, 'Do you really think you can manage a half marathon in the rain with a full bladder?'

'Actually, he makes a decent point,' my imaginary angel conceded. And so, the decision was made.

I ditched the running pack and rushed towards a free space off track. In doing so I heard Formula 1 commentator David Croft in my head shouting, 'Oh look here! Warren's gone off the track and is heading towards the barriers!' Followed by Martin Brundle adding, 'He's pissing up the wall Crofty!' 30 seconds later, I ran on feeling much lighter with absolutely no regrets.

Finding a rhythm

Due to my gentle pace, the early miles felt like the longest of my life. I kept it in my head that this was all part of the process and that I would know when it was time to turn up the tempo. I relied on training run experience for reassurance that it would take slightly longer to feel comfortable. My previous long runs only felt pleasant after roughly the fourth mile, so I issued an ultimatum to all my current discomforts, for which I had many.

Firstly, that damn pasta was *still* tumbling around in my stomach and I began dreading the inevitable stitch. Secondly, my shoelaces were perhaps too tight, because my entire right foot was going numb with pins and needles.[23] There was little I could do

---

[23] This is a common issue- especially when you use insoles- suggesting your shoelaces are too tight.

other than keep going and hope the blood would return; mental preparations were however made to cross the finish line with only one foot. Thirdly, and on the subject of feet, mine were soaked. The rain had properly picked up leaving all of us open to the elements. Soon, puddles began to form and inevitably I accidentally stepped in all of them. My basic running shoes weren't designed to repel puddles of water and so I had to brace for the sensation of cold water seeping through my socks and into both feet- at this point I was glad I could only feel one of them.

The opening few miles certainly weren't very comfortable, what with one of my feet about to drop off and the other likely to get trench foot. However, all these minor inconveniences were dwarfed by the sheer sense of trial and adventure. I navigated famous corners and then tight bottleneck twists behind the track. Every step of the way I ran alongside fellow runners, who like me had put in the preparation, no doubt gone through their own setbacks along the way, and now were here with me on this very day to cross the same finish line. Those of us that did finish would all cross at different times and get there in different ways; there were slow and steady runners like me and then there were the run-walkers. One old lady in particular would walk leisurely for a while, drop behind me, and then come steaming past like shit off a shovel every five minutes. It was mildly entertaining amidst this bitterly cold morning.

However, the weather soon picked up and so did my pace. Both took a while, but by being patient I reaped the rewards at long last. By the fifth mile I had spent the entire hour being overtaken by thousands and thousands of people. No lie- the entire field just took off at a different speed despite all of us being organised into predicted finish time groups on the start grid. Although this didn't bother me, it sure felt satisfying once my pace naturally clicked into something a little more 'competitive' shall we say. Now please trust me on this one, because I am adamant in saying that no matter what kind of running event you enter the true competition is always with yourself... But I absolutely bloody loved it when I started hoovering up the half-distance bottlers after the 6-mile mark. For those that had expended all their energy at the start, they were about to get passed by a rainbow in tights.

Before I knew it, the blood had returned to my right foot, my feet had dried under the kind sun, and the pasta had at long last been converted into energy! The blue touch paper was well and truly lit and off I raced. The next few miles were the best I had ever run in my life. Everything was coming together; each step felt effortless and the quicker pace hardly required any more energy. I began eyeing up unknowing 'rivals' in the far distance and grew in speed and confidence as they drew nearer. This was the closest I've ever felt to flying as I navigated the circuit's many corners and accelerated past everyone in sight. Finally, my patience was coming into fruition- this is where the run really started.

At certain mile-markers there were Lucozade drinks stations, so I took full advantage by taking a bottle and keeping it with me for a few cheeky sips whenever needed. I don't exactly know what they put in that stuff, but it was enough to turbocharge me to find levels of pace that I previously only thought possible during tempo or interval runs. I could not believe the pace- since when was this in my locker? I ran quicker than I had ever done in training yet still felt like I was on autopilot- it just goes to show that your mind and body do react in different and confusing ways.

In the morning and at the start of the race, my body was tense and hesitant compared to my mind which was raring to go. Now, despite my mind still being firmly focussed on finding the finish, my body had galloped ahead and found unprecedented levels of performance. The two were now in unison, attacking the same mission and the results were remarkable. I knew full well however that it was now the job of my mind to reign in my body, just as the mile 8 barrier came into view. Now we were into the unknown, a distance we (mind and body) had never covered before. Many runners had lost the mental battle and compromised their bodies earlier in the run and many more would do so from now on. It was my job to stay disciplined to prevent running the tank dry.

Into the unknown

What would happen hereafter? I wondered how my body would cope, knowing full well that maintaining this ever-increasing pace could spell recipe for disaster. Mile 8 felt good as ever, but by mile 9 I knew my energy levels were about to start dropping. I made the wise decision to put the brakes on to save whatever remained at the end for a strong finish. The finish line photo sat firmly in the back of my mind- got to make sure I cross the line looking noble. I don't think I would've been able to post a social media update after if I was depicted crawling on my knees with bloodshot eyes in utter agony.

By this point many runners began tragically crashing out of the event. I passed an increasing number of runners sat on the sidelines with their shoes off looking dejected; some had first aid members comforting them, while some desperately stretched and massaged their injured areas in hopes of continuing. Some runners pulled to the less busy side of the track and gingerly hobbled with one hand on the back of a hamstring, many of whom looked to be seasoned runners with skinny, streamlined bodies and the names of their running clubs written in capitals on their vests. While some of these injuries were probably acute, it just goes to show that the saying applies to all of us: failure to prepare means preparing to fail.

As the bodies kept dropping, I cautiously ran on, amazed at how many were pulling out of the race. Was everyone just pushing too hard? Was it the cold and rain at the start? I wasn't sure. But at this rate it wouldn't have surprised me if all of us staggered to the line knees locked and screaming in pain like a pack of uncoordinated zombies.

'Keep your head Ellis, you too could be side-lined if you get too ambitious again,' remained the revolving wisdom needed to safely guide me through as I hit double-digit miles for the first time ever. Now I was beginning to feel my legs grow heavy. Now it was getting hard. Now I anticipated the mental battle. I had been waiting for this a very long time, ever since I set out on that first ever run on New Year's Day, I had anticipated the gruelling mental battle. I wanted to feel the urge to stop and go against it. I wanted to grapple with myself and prove that I possessed the mental fortitude to continue through physical pain and not back down from a challenge. I wished to discipline myself to the finish and complete what I had set out to achieve. Above all, I wished to put everything I had learnt since that first run to the test and prove to that lonely, low self-esteem teenager that he is capable of overcoming his weaknesses and sticking it out to the finish.

I welcomed the final three miles. I wanted them to be as hard as possible and I got my wish. Miles 11 and 12 were where the legs really started to seize up; sips of Lucozade became gulps in a bid to ignite one last sugar rush to the end. My main goal was to keep running and finish without stopping. Once I stopped to walk it would be over as from then on, I believed my body would allow itself to subsequently repeat this 'backing down' behaviour. No, I wanted to instil a *need* to continue through developing the ability to ignore those false inner calls to quit.

Sure enough, those calls to quit did indeed arrive with increasing urgency and now I felt very uncomfortable. I found myself seeking the mile markers so often that time seemed to slow down. The support however remained relentless. The crowds continued to cheer, the marshals kept up their encouragement, the camaraderie between fellow runners urging each other on remained intact and grew stronger through these harsh final miles. The music grew louder, signifying that the finish line neared. Pacers checked their watches and the huffing and puffing of bodies all around me grew more strained. This is where we really find out our limits.

We reached the final mile where I decided to ditch my Lucozade bottle- which had felt quite heavy for the past few miles- and hopefully stick it out to the finish. This however, turned into what is undoubtedly the most embarrassing moment I have ever experienced at a running event. In an attempt to throw my Lucozade bottle to the side of the track, I used the momentum from the propelling swing of my right arm to create the motion that would aim the bottle's trajectory to the side, out of harm's way. However, as I made the swing with my arm, my hand mysteriously lost the ability to let go of its tight grip on the bottle. Due to my fatigue at that point, the energy exerted to make the swing followed through with such vigour that when I did finally let go of the bottle, I sent it soaring high up into the sky, directly above the heads of hundreds of runners around me. I looked up in horror at the small, half-full missile I had unintentionally launched.

'Heads!', cried a shaky voice from behind as the crowds immediately dispersed. The bottle came crashing down, falling like a dead weight. I couldn't possibly bear to turn around and watch the impending doom- just keep running and they might not notice it was me. As I sensed it nearing its collision with Earth, I heard screams and shrieks of terror before the unthinkable happened. Once the bottle made contact with the tarmac, the cap dislodged ever so slightly from the neck, causing a fizzy reaction of epic proportions. Like a firework, the bottle shot across the track, wiping out four runners in merciless succession before finishing off the fifth by showering them in Lucozade and smacking them around the kisser. Then, in horrific but also quite comical style, the bottle began whizzing around the track like a balloon ridding itself of air, and knocked down every runner in sight like dominoes. Roughly after the event's 2-hour mark, no runners were registered to have finished.

… Okay, some of that might have not happened and my mind may have gotten slightly carried away. The coffee appears to be kicking in as I sit here and type this. What actually happened was the bottle hit the ground with a tremendous heavy slap, but fortunately no one got hurt. Everyone probably thought I was a right dickhead though afterwards. Sorry guys.

With the disaster over and having been liberated from my weapon of mass destruction, I pressed forward with the finish line drawing nearer. Ironically, it would now be a case of not bottling it before the finish.

My legs groaned at each stride, growing heavier and heavier, I utilised my arms more for added propulsion and kept my breathing in check as instructed by dear Adriene. I knew I could do it, I knew I would reach the end, but at the same time I wished the finish line would get its arse in gear and show itself because I felt pretty certain that my legs would crumble at any moment.

For an infinite number of minutes, the name of the game was one foot in front of the other, two sharp breaths in and two lazy and weak breaths out. My body raged with pain, my mind screamed to stop, but my willpower reminded me to have faith in both, stick to the techniques, and keep moving. Soon, that faith was finally rewarded, as there in the distance waiting at the end of a long left-hander lie the finish line in its humungous glory. The grandstands were packed for the finish, spectators lined both sides of the home straight. The goal was there, the finish in sight.

A true sense of accomplishment

No chance of backing down now. Once on the home straight I gazed ahead at the large arching finish-line stand welcoming me with open arms. The charge began. With all my remaining energy, I conjured up the strength to break into a sprint, powering my arms and legs with the very last kilojoule of energy available. I sped up as fast as I could go, giving it my all, leaving no ounce of willpower unused in this painful last dash.

The finish line drew nearer, but for the first time in my life I came face to face with my own physical limit. This wasn't related to pain tolerance at all; in that moment my lungs just could not withstand the demand any further. My throat seized up and no air passed through. Now I'm not asthmatic, but this was a complete first- all I knew was that I had pushed myself harder than I had ever done before and found my body's absolute highest level of tolerance for it. Fortunately, the sprint was timed well enough to just about make it to the line without suffocating.

With a punch to the air and a cheek to cheek smile, I crossed the line to complete my first ever half marathon.

Absolute jubilation. As I slowed to a pleasant walking speed, someone placed an amazing medal around my neck, handed me a special finishers' T-shirt, and then a goodie bag full of snacks to kickstart my recovery. What luxury! It was a welcome to the finishers' club fit for royalty. After performing a few warm down stretches, I peered into my goodies and gazed at my new medal with loving eyes.

This was my *first* running medal, and to this day is one of the most special. I still have it hanging up directly above my bed. I had a few medals from my days playing football for my primary school, but they were undated and were only designed with a generic photo of some boots and a ball. This running medal was everything I wanted; it was golden with a unique tyre design, had 'Adidas Silverstone Half Marathon 2017' written on it alongside the date of the special milestone: Sunday 12th March 2017.[24]

Once I returned to the paddock I sought to reunite with Dad, hoping he got a cool video of me crossing the line. However, he was nowhere to be seen. For about 20 minutes I walked up and down the grounds, asking marshals if they had seen a dapper looking geezer but to no avail. Feeling a bit like a lost child in the supermarket, I hurried off to the stands to see if he was around there. Then, on my way past the finish line, I saw my old man standing with an intense, fixed gaze at the mass crowd of runners finishing their race- the numpty had only completely missed the moment I crossed the line. I snuck behind and gave him an almighty surprise. Laughing, he said, 'I thought something 'ad 'appened to ya!' in cheerful cockney. We had a good chuckle and

---

[24] The medal was so special to me that it became the subject of my 'show and tell' presentation in Japanese class. I told the story of my battle to get it and received the highest grade! Afterwards, it hung proudly from the pinboard in my university room. A well-hung medal indeed.

headed to the paddock, where I could at last change into some warmer clothes.

I kicked off my running shoes and socks for the first time in over two hours and my goodness me were my feet a sight. Having soaked up the rainwater and retained it amongst the sweat, the results were rather unsightly. Dad was used to cutting up raw fish for his job on a daily basis, but even he remarked that they looked a bit clapped. I covered them up with a thick and warm pair of socks and slipped on my lovely finishers' shirt. I then cracked open a protein shake and welcomed the most insane runner's high ever. For the rest of the day I would feel euphoric. And I had all the reason to; in this sensational week I had made two first-class presentations, completed my second essay in two weeks, and raised over £350 for Rainbow Trust by running my first ever half marathon. Without running, goodness knows what I would have been doing instead.

Once we hit the road for the return journey, a growl from both our stomachs took us to a roadside Burger King, where I had the fattest bacon cheeseburger on the menu. Inside, Dad and I sat by the roadside watching the hundreds of cars race past on the motorway and spoke about one day doing an event together.

I can safely say that that meal was one of the most satisfying of my entire life up to that point. What's more, many other runners had joined us with the same initiative. My blog perfectly captured the atmosphere:

'The double bacon cheeseburger I had was like it had been prepared from heaven's grill itself, yet the most amusing aspect was bumping into fellow runners afterwards. We all proudly donned our finishers' T-shirts and medals, yet all walked like we had no function left in our legs. We'd make eye contact, and just laugh. There was a mutual understanding; a general relief and sense of achievement. We were all on a massive high. Everything just felt so rewarding.'[25]

Night had fallen by the time Dad dropped me back at the halls and we parted ways. He spoke of how proud he felt of me out there, and we left each other with the thought of one day challenging a full marathon together. Whatever the future held I couldn't wait- I had completely fallen in love with running.

The jubilation from what was a truly memorable day remained strong through the night. I would later receive professional photos immortalising the pain and emotion of completing my first half. I would also receive a cool cut-out desk trophy from Rainbow Trust accompanied with a letter personally thanking me for my fundraising efforts.

After blogging my exciting day, I lay in bed, happily aching. Yes, tomorrow would be Monday and another essay awaited, but before this remarkable week was up, I took a moment to reflect on the journey up until now. All the ups and downs culminated with this achievement. I gazed at my medal with delight and felt immense pride. So many lessons learnt, so much effort and heartache for this medal commemorating my first ever half marathon. I then became quite busy on my phone, telling my

---

[25] https://elliswarrensite.wordpress.com/2017/03/16/adidas-silverstone-half-marathon-2017/

friends- old and new- the story of the amazing day and how I couldn't wait for the next event.

Weeks like this are rare- but once every so often a plan goes perfectly well, and you are given a glimpse of the wonders you can achieve. I finally knew that I *did* have the mental strength- the willpower- to pull myself through when times became testing. I could finally accept that I am not lazy, I am not weak, and I am not a loser! I *do* have fight in me. I *am* capable. It had taken so long to reach this point, and that, I believe, was the greatest achievement from the entire week.

What a wonderful journey these past three months had been. That night, I went to bed a very happy man.

Chapter 10
The runner's life

Back to business. From now on the next target was the marathon. I approached the next stage of training humbled- completing a half was tough enough, now I had to double the distance.

Two months remained until the marathon; this meant exams loomed closer too. Following the half, the four-week essay slog finally met its finale prompting great relief. Completing the mammoth workload only felt better at the end of term when all my classmates frantically scrambled to meet their deadlines.

From this point onwards, I would apply the finish touches to the grand projects that were the marathon and exam attempts. There was plenty of hard work still to be done with revision and long runs, but now completion was so near I could almost taste that first celebratory beer. Even though so much work still remained, I felt as if the hardest parts of the process were behind me now, because I eagerly looked forward to grafting through the final stages of my endeavours. It no longer felt like work.

In essence, the hard days were over. From now on, every additional step towards the end goal would be celebratory. Why? Because I already realised the extent of what this running journey had done for me.

In this chapter I will explain every merit from becoming a runner. You may notice I have decided to detail the merits *before* we even reach the final goal of the marathon. The reason for this is because by this point in the journey that 'end goal' now felt like the additional icing on the cake, a sexy velvet cake that already tasted damn delicious.

The marathon would signify the crowning moment, the extra golden glimmer of an already completed goal, the Flandre to your Embodiment of Scarlet Devil- you could say it even started to feel like a bonus. Back when I set my goals in chapter 2, I could have never guessed how fulfilled I might feel even before the journey's great climax. To my surprise, what I gained before even reaching the marathon start line felt like the main reward, a reward so empowering and great and memorable.

That reward was the journey. This running journey- in which I first set foot as a complete beginner- encompassed rapid success on a deeply personal level. It bungeed my mental health up to new levels of resilience, taught me to plan for success, and opened my mind up to discover so much about the world as well as myself. It even gave a new, fresh look on my identity. As a 19-year-old lad still finding his way in the world, this felt like a massive revelation. Yet when it comes to running, age is arbitrary. There is no age limit to experience the growth and improvements that running can encourage. If you simply set a goal and run towards it with an open and honest mind, then believe me, you could be about to pen one of the greatest chapters in your life so far.

Empowerment for mental health

The running journey encompasses many positive spill-over effects, but for many of us running and mental health are closely linked. As discussed previously, relying exclusively on running to maintain our mental health is not wise, because setbacks to running become setbacks to our mood and productivity. Instead, utilising running as a powerful tool particularly when times get tough will provide the instant mood booster, the short-term *and* long-term sense of accomplishment, the big goal to look forward to, and the journey to enjoy along the way.

After learning to use running as a routine-creating tool of empowerment, I can fully say that I *learnt* how to rid myself of the dark cloud hovering over my head since the start of university. Every morning the sense of routine from running combined with the feeling that I was taking more precious steps towards something much greater gave me a reason to leap out of bed and get cracking on another busy day. This also helped reframe other aspects of my life, namely university. What previously felt like an endless quest without reward now had structure; by breaking each year down and then further organising my academic and career goals by the term, suddenly there was merit to my efforts at the end- everything fit together like a jigsaw because creating the best 'you' is a piecemeal process.

Thanks to running, I always had something to look forward to- tomorrow was always worth waking up for and the future always worth seeing. Long-term goal setting became my window into greater times ahead. If planning for the long term feels like a hopeless task to you, and you genuinely start to believe that the future is not worth living for, then let's reframe the process: All that's required is the slightest bit of curiosity, the smallest morsel of intrigue that makes you wonder what will happen further down the line. This is the key to emerging from rock bottom. Running gave me that curiosity, because it asked a very interesting question: 'Six months down the line from now will you be able to run a marathon?' And with the marathon officially confirmed I could also ponder, 'Will you feel better about yourself by then?' I wanted to know- I knew it was well worth knowing. And so I ventured forward into the curious unknown.

Obviously, there were times when I felt down and stressed with work. That doesn't change, I'm afraid. But the difference is that I knew what to do. During setbacks, we have to release pent up energy- negative energy to be precise. Whether that's through a fast, high-intensity run or a slow gentle pace that allows you to verbally vent anything- a venture into the outdoors is what disconnects you from the darkness clouding your mind and reconnects you with your body. Not to mention the runner's high almost always ensures you return home feeling positive, and much better for having gone out.

Socially sound

By the time I finished my first term at university, I would definitely say that I lost my social swagger. The energy and the wit which I loved to share with everyone vanished. My confidence was shot, and I became a hollow version of the bright and optimistic lad that collected his A-levels and left school; the boy who won 'Happiest Person in the Year' in sixth form was seemingly dead.

By the time I returned to that same school to collect my certificates two months into university, my old teachers probably wondered what had happened. I couldn't engage comfortably with anyone, felt too awkward to hold a conversation and stumbled over my words when asked how university was going. I could not generate a socially acceptable and positive answer because I had no words capable of justifying my situation. I felt like everything had to be justified, as if there was an excuse for feeling unhappy, which of course you can't express over small talk. Returning to school was really embarrassing.

I became a different person again the following spring, but this time for the better. Whether it be family, friends, potential new friends, acquaintances, or complete strangers- I could comfortably converse because I now felt content with myself and who I was. I had clear goals and was heading in a bright direction- no longer did I feel like a fraud, hiding under imposter syndrome on campus or at the dinner table.

Once back home for Easter I could confidently maintain eye contact with whoever I spoke with and no longer crumbled under a sense of inferiority. I had my own identity, my own goals, and ambitions and for that reason I felt like a functional human being once again. Released from the safety net of compulsory education, my wellbeing and success was now entirely my responsibility, and that felt liberating. Having struggled to claim that responsibility and instead frame it as increased pressure, I unknowingly clung on to a teenager's mindset in an adult world.

Back in London for the final term and where I once felt lost in the maize of faces, I now saw opportunity. I now knew how to pick out like-minded individuals who strived to be better; friendships and connections of the sort are hard to find and take time to develop but are undoubtedly worthwhile. As I got to know master's and PhD students in my Japanese class, I soon became welcome in their circles. They say you are the product of the people around you and boy did I feel lucky with these fellas. It may have taken over three quarters of the academic year, but the wait was worthwhile. We used to play basketball at the park opposite the halls and then grab lunch together every week. As a short and skinny white boy, you probably wouldn't expect me to be any good at basketball, and of course you'd be right- I was bloody awful.

But that mattered very little- sitting around people who were a bit older and a little bit ahead of the game proved ever so insightful, and for any reader- regardless of age- I cannot stress just how stimulating it is to sit and listen to people you admire. Just by immersing yourself in an ambitious set of people you will feel inclined to aim high yourself. I considered each and every one of them a level of intelligence above me, (and that's not just the imposter syndrome talking) and valued the time spent hearing what goes through their minds. One of them even had a credit card solely for the purpose of improving their credit score- this amazed me, because up until that point I had only seen my mates back home use them to buy turbo-charged German saloons which they couldn't afford.

Had I met those gentlemen back in the first term then perhaps the friendship wouldn't have worked out. I would've felt too inferior, and if we're being honest, a bit too envious to stick around. Now though, I knew the willpower to overcome weaknesses would more than compensate for any academic shortcomings. I knew that if you work smart and hard, then you can confidently stand alongside any of your peers because once exams arrived, I saw first-hand how hard and active workers triumph over lazy prodigies.

Aiming for academic excellence

By the time we reached the exam term, familiar but not so fond faces in my courses began to disappear. In fact, all across the university, first year students were giving up and dropping out in large numbers. I felt slightly perplexed that the few people I shared small talk with before and after lectures had all decided university wasn't for them. All of them were now gone- I wondered if I was the problem, and if me rambling on about running every week was the final nail in the coffin for them. I should hope not, because for most of them the problem was with themselves.

Having grown up in a cash-strapped secondary school, I became accustomed to a supportive and humble environment when it came to academic performance. While the camaraderie between my 150 brothers and sisters of my secondary school year group gifted a memorable adolescence, it couldn't prepare me for the raging egos one can expect at higher education. As I alluded to in chapter 1, the arrogance and entitlement of a lot of people proved a nasty shock. By the time the first round of essay grades came out in the economics department, I sat in a tutorial full of whinging spoilt kids accusing the tutor of marking too harshly and failing to understand the meaning of their arguments. He replied that the content was adequate, but the presentation and structure was all over the place. They ignored that feedback and lobbied for reconsideration, failing to comprehend that there were areas beyond content that required hard work. They failed to realise that their natural grasp of the academic history of economics alone would not suffice to write a good essay.

When the next essays came back, they received the same feedback and the same arguments raged once more. A term later, most of them had packed up and taken their tuition fees and higher education privileges elsewhere. These people are slaves to their EELs, the lethal triad of excuses, ego, and laziness that we talked about in chapter 2. As you can see, what happened was their egos believed they were beyond any constructive criticism, their arrogance ignored it, and their damaged motivation combined with zero willpower convinced them that seeking pastures new would solve their problem. All they did was waste their time and [parents'] money. The likelihood is they'll repeat the same frustrations and never know why.

The lesson here applies to the working world as well as university. Self-entitled tossers don't have the tenacity to better themselves and for that reason remain endlessly unfulfilled and deluded off a toxic bitterness.

I managed to avoid entering this cycle of bitter resentment by realising that as a person and as an academic, I needed serious work. Just like when reflecting on my long-term struggle to run, I took my mental defence barriers down and admitted my academic flaws: my writing style appeared unprofessional, my depth of analysis lacking, my explanation of points missing, the list was extensive. It was running that encouraged me to humbly realise and accept those shortcomings, flaws, and underdeveloped attributes which could be improved with smart work. No longer did I need to be naturally good at something to achieve success at it; no matter how incapable we are from the outset, hard work and dedication can still produce remarkable success, and running is proof of that. As I've said time and time again, running taught me to overcome my weaknesses by planning, experimenting with what works, and striving to see each task to completion. It helped me utilise flashcards as my main method of revision and create long-term strategies that organised how to attack each goal. Talent does not come into it.

The consequence of not admitting I needed to improve was failing academically and then probably surrendering my place at university through a lack of self-belief. The gain for actively trying to improve was earning a first-class grade on every assignment, meeting mature and poised-for-success friends, and of course, owning the physical and mental ability to run a marathon coupled with the growth and willpower-driven mindset to overcome any obstacle. The decision to work on your flaws therefore shouldn't be a hard one.

Towards the end goals

The third and final term, the 'exam term' of the academic year would play host to the grand finale of my New Year's goals. Armed with over four-hundred handwritten flashcards, I knew exactly what I needed to do for a first and exactly how to go about it. As for running, with the weekly mileage increasing and Sunday long runs reaching 20 miles, I now needed a bit more than just a pair of running shoes.

To be fully prepared for the marathon, I would need to conquer 20-mile long runs by learning how to manage my nutrition and hydration to ensure I wouldn't hit the infamous Wall before the end. Your body cannot store enough glycogen (the stuff that gives your muscles energy) past mile 20, so a drastic drop in performance is almost certain.

For those wondering, the Wall is so feared because in its worst scenarios, it can leave you stumbling around wondering where you are, much like your nan after she's had too many sherries at a wedding reception. I'm sure we've all seen the viral videos of marathon runners collapsing. Picture that, and then imagine yourself crawling around Hyde Park while a group of tourists eat up their free half hour on the Boris bikes just to watch in bemusement. That should provide a decent incentive to steer clear of the Wall.

I learnt of the need to take on 'fuel' mid-run once I ventured over 15 miles. I read up online and saw a whole marketplace full of quirky energy bars and chews to provide you with an ample amount of carbohydrates. You can of course invest in the high-end products specifically made for athletes, but if you're on a budget then do remember that these kinds of products don't do anything that a good old flapjack or bag of jelly babies won't. For on-the-go energy that's easy to consume and digest, you want to get a pack of gels. I bought a small box from Amazon which contained enough for four weeks' worth of long runs. Take one each hour and you'll have that extra bit of oomph needed to keep powering forward. Some of the gels even contain caffeine and boy does it make you go like the clappers.

Studying different nutrition strategies that play with what you should consume provided great background knowledge for when I eventually formed my own. Once again, the key is to experiment and find what works for you. For example, almost any running nutrition guide you'll read happily suggests bananas prior to a workout and sometimes even during it. However, my experiences with them have never been good. For starters, running with a load of bananas strapped to my belt is awkward and obviously attracts gorillas, plus keeping them in a bag turns them black, resulting in a load of horrible squidgy banana oozing inside and ruining the whole bag- nasty. Then there's actually digesting them, and to this day I haven't eaten a banana without it repeating on me throughout the entire run. It's safe to say bananas and I don't agree, but for you they might be magic fuel.

On the other hand, a lot of people say they hate gels, and to be honest I haven't met a single person who genuinely likes them, but for me they are delicious gourmet meals for when I'm powering around Hyde Park. They come in all sorts of nice flavours and are easy to digest, although I suppose once your mouth is gagging for some kind of substance that's when they taste best. For me it's always a refreshing relief and never have they given me gastro problems *during* a run; when I visit the toilet afterwards, mind you, it's a 'long' story in every sense of the word.

With regards to hydration, I learnt the hard way. When the smallest hint of summer weather teased the nation, I supposed that my 17-mile long run would simply be a sweatier affair than usual and resultingly found another area of great naïveté. 12 miles into my first ever run above 20 degrees Celsius (don't laugh non-UK readers, it was like an oven) and the intense heat that had slowly built up since the beginning melted below my skin, creating a new sensation that felt worryingly peculiar. For all the heat I had just endured, now I felt cold. A chill spread across my body and a pressure caved in my stomach and throat. Breathing became laborious. My legs also grew heavier and each step became heavy and exhausted more energy than before. The sun glared down from a cloudless sky and completely baked me. Red-faced and gasping for increasingly futile gulps of air, my mind experienced a mild panic that invited an influx of thoughts.

At first, I shrugged it off as another mental game where I had to fight off the repeated screams of 'stop!'. This battle turned out different to the others; I felt unable to escape from the constant urges from my mind while trying to push through the 17 miles. The pure mental chaos made each second pass like a minute and each minute drag like an hour. I couldn't focus. Everything ached. Everything cried for me to stop. No air could satisfy my lungs, no decline could ease my legs, and certainly no mantra nor grit could deter this mental anguish. My heart thumped against my chest. I felt cold, sick, and as if everything was about to fail internally. Now, I started listening to those calls to stop and allowed the idea to manifest. Yeah, perhaps a brief walk would reset the pain? Maybe I was going too fast? Total bollocks.

I was experiencing cardiac drift- the steady increase in heartrate despite maintaining a constant pace due to a rise in my body's core temperature and a loss of water.[26] Basically, I was massively dehydrated. This came to my knowledge during post run analysis and changed my view at the time which was that I had merely been a pussy. On occasions such as these, your body is doing you a massive favour. Even now, I have to teach myself how to distinguish tenacity from being a tit. Water is a vital part of a successful long run, especially in hot conditions. Overlooking it will guarantee you a disappointing performance and potentially fainting, not to mention the possibility of experiencing some whacky hallucinations- I once again invite you to picture such an outcome at Hyde Park, where you'll probably conclude your run in the back of a police car.

With summer coming early I thus dedicated my final long runs of training to mastering the art of eating and drinking while on

---

[26] https://www.polar.com/blog/cardiac-drift-effect-on-training

the move. At first, my stomach sulked at having to multitask, but eventually we nailed a comfortable strategy. I felt disappointed and eager to reconciliate following the 17-miler but bounced back in buoyant style a week later. I felt nervous about attempting 20 miles in similar conditions, but with the right fuelling and refuelling strategy, the big two-zero became another successfully completed milestone.

An hour before the run, I ate a nice bowl of oatmeal and consumed a couple glasses of water, then during the three-and-a-bit hours outside I took a gel each hour, sneaked a couple of jelly babies in between, and sipped on water roughly every 25 minutes. Carrying a water bottle around didn't seem practical until I found one shaped so that you have a handle built into the bottle- you hold a bit less water, but the ergonomic gains more than make up for it. Thanks to this relatively basic strategy, I ran the 20-miler at a faster average pace than the 17 and completed it without having to stop- in fact, it felt easier! I even felt like there could possibly be more in the tank, but of course we don't go beyond what the grand plan tells us, or we risk compromising the rest of the journey.

Mastering refuelling proved to be one more challenge I had to overcome to reach the 20+ mile distance. Others included breathing techniques, stride length, but there are many better books out there for mastering the finer arts. Keeping things basic, my routine throughout the period where exam revision and 20+ mile training runs was as follows:

1. Wake up at 7:30am
2. Begin warming up at 9am
3. Run/yoga/gym
4. Lunch at 12pm
5. Class/revision
6. Dinner at 6pm
7. Revision
8. Bed by 11:30pm

It's a simple look at things, but a simple routine is easier to follow. The main gist is to exercise in the mornings and then go hard on the work for the rest of the day. I allowed myself generous breaks on the condition that I completed the tasks set on my planner. Once my daily tasks were complete, e.g. practice exam questions for term 1 weeks 3-6 on microeconomics, I allowed myself the freedom after to do whatever I fancied, even if that meant bingeing on YouTube. Productivity was therefore incentivised and rewarded. The routine worked for every day except Sundays, where I really recommend just giving yourself a well-deserved break, especially after a long run. When I completed my 20-milers my head was all over the place from general fatigue. Give yourself the day off; I spent my whole time lounging in bed watching films. Disconnecting briefly from your intense focus on a goal can do wonders in avoiding burnout.

Ready to rumble

Were there days when I didn't feel as excited about getting out of bed and running? Were there days when I just didn't feel like working? Yes, and yes. Of course there were. Did those feelings affect me? Absolutely not. Remember, we no longer rely on motivation. Motivation comes and goes, it's the most unreliable emotion you'll ever experience. We don't need it. At this point, my daily productivity was driven purely by willpower, which is the key underlying element that denotes every success in this book. Running and willpower have a mutually beneficial relationship; running creates stronger willpower, and willpower improves your mental capabilities as a runner. Running creates a positive, 'can-do' attitude, encouraging you to pour more ambition into your career and working life, while willpower allows you to sustain it.

Thanks to willpower, I could prevent my mind's whinging from sabotaging my body's capabilities. Those groggy mornings were weathered by clearing my mind of any negative thoughts and simply acting. Just act. Act first and the positive thoughts will follow. You will always feel better after a run that you initially felt unenthusiastic about.

If you are committed to running a marathon- or any goal for that matter- make it your duty to shift into gear and complete that task because procrastination is simply not an option.

By the time running 20-milers had become comfortable, my 13 weeks of intensive training had finished, and I had now entered a fortnight of 'tapering', whereby the mileage would drastically lower to allow me to recover and feel fresh in time for the marathon. Similarly, by the time all my revision flashcards were memorised and all potential exam questions covered, the real exams were now just around the corner. It was showtime.

After all the preparation and lessons learnt along the way, the climactic moment of truth had finally arrived. I knew I was ready. I had overcome the setbacks, the temptation to quit, and the hardest hurdles that trip up all of us along the way. I was still standing, still healthy, and still with my eyes firmly on the prize.

The marathon would be another family day out, this time with Mum and Nan. I would take the train from London to stay at Nan's house for a few nights, before meeting Mum and making the short 10-minute journey down the road to the circuit. I harboured a serious sense of purpose pulling my suitcase through the gates at St Pancras; it felt like my first ever business trip, taking the high-speed service for my duel with destiny. Never had a visit to my nan's house been so serious.

On marathon week, I upped my intake of carbohydrates and electrolytes, preparing for what was meant to be a scorcher at the weekend: high humidity and temperatures nearing 30 degrees. I didn't feel worried at all, and that was for two reasons. Firstly, I had already experienced dehydration in my training runs and learnt how to survive and thrive in hot weather. The weather could get as hot as it liked, because I knew what to expect; I knew how tough and uncomfortable it would feel, and so there would be no surprises. I would know exactly how to react.

Secondly, whatever the situation and whatever the conditions, I knew I had the willpower to get myself to that finish line one way or another. It didn't matter if during the race one of my legs broke or all those electrolytes finally caught up on my bowels, I was set on finishing and was therefore prepared to do whatever it took. I strongly believed that I had the willpower to overcome any discomfort thrown at me. The goal was to finish. Therefore, I could run, walk, crawl, cha cha slide, anything. It didn't matter because I was already visualising exactly how sweet crossing the line would be.

Above all, I believed in myself because I had already succeeded in completing the hardest part of the journey. I made it to the start line. And, I made it in the best shape of my life, ready to run a full marathon. Yes, the true achievement was making it to the start line and the true reward was the journey. What followed would be a further celebration of those efforts.

Chapter 11
Marathon day: No challenge greater

5:30am: Time to rise and shine; it was marathon day. The sun exhaled its first hot breath of the morning and immediately I awoke. My alarm was poised to go off any moment now, yet my spooky knack for waking up mere minutes before an alarm is due to sound came clutch once again. Nan too had awoken and was raring to go, having already spent a couple of hours sitting in bed munching on a bowl of cereal- this woman gets ahead of the game.

The temperature steadily climbed into heatwave conditions without a cloud in the sky- forget the sunscreen at your own peril. I woke early to take on an energy packed breakfast. My usual Weetabix was replaced with a couple of slices of toast, a banana, a flapjack, an electrolyte drink, and a few jelly babies- perhaps you can tell why I wanted an early start.

Once Mum arrived, we headed off to the venue early to get warmed up. The Kent Circuit Marathon would be a significantly smaller event than the Silverstone Half, with 400 runners registered to participate. However, we would all share the same 1.3-mile circuit for 20 laps, so no one would get lonely out there.

At reception, the staff had obviously been awake for a while as the energy in the room was contagious, especially when the esteemed and well-loved regular runners of that particular event organisation turned up. The small-scale nature of the event evoked a sense of community; even though I knew absolutely none of the other runners and appeared an outcast, the friendly atmosphere made it easy to spring up a few chats.

I learnt that the regulars of this organisation's events were more local and quite frankly, remarkable individuals. As I collected my vest designed especially for this event by the organisers, I looked around to see older ladies and gentlemen sporting their 'Marathon 100 Club' vests, with many other special shirts commemorating 'x marathons in x months'. 'Blimey,' I thought, 'A *hundred*?! That's absolute madness!' While I pluckily lined up to run my first ever marathon, I would stand alongside people who had run *hundreds*; a staggering realisation, one that revealed the different dimension of running I had unknowingly discovered.

Once registration was complete, Mum set up a base by the side of the circuit while Nan and I popped off for a quick view of the course. A cavalry of dark clouds had begun to charge in from the west, threatening to eclipse the harsh sunlight. While a bit of shielding from the sun wouldn't go amiss, I sensed that if rubbed the wrong way those clouds would absolutely drench us out there.

I welcomed the combination of angry skies and high humidity and the roaring gigantic sun looming above. I wanted all the elements to present their worst. Bring on the tsunamis, the spontaneous fires, and the earthquakes I say! Give me the worst you can conjure! Okay, let's not get too carried away- high heat and humidity is extraordinary enough by Kent standards. I just wanted the hardest test possible for the 5-month journey's finale.

As the start time drew nearer, I arranged all the gels in my running belt (basically a bum bag) and laid out a few bottles of water in positions where I could easily grab them whilst running past. I also placed twenty-one elastic bands around my wrist; they were handed out during registration for the sole purpose of keeping track of what lap I was on. They reminded me a bit of those 'shag bands' that used to be trendy back in school, although thankfully there were no forfeits for breaking these ones.

Mum and Nan got comfy on a couple of folding chairs and made sure to apply generous amounts of sunscreen before they busted out the biscuits. They would need it, given that my estimated finishing time meant they could be sat outside way into the day's hottest hours, possibly all the way through to the evening if things got tough.

At 8:50am, it was time to line up on the starting grid. I genuinely believed nothing could stop me. No distance would be too far, no heat too hot, and no hill too high; I really believed I would make it to the finish. Finally, the gentleman with the starting gun shot a hole through one of the clouds and initiated the beginning of our 26.2 mile run to glory. He also gave the heavy and ever darkening clouds above their prompt to attack, and with uncanny timing, ten-pence sized spots of rain began to fall around the circuit. I was about to undergo a trial like no other.

A soggy but solid start

The pack's slow edging towards the start line once again triggered that race-start adrenaline that catches out so many. I saw most jump at the opportunity to charge off into the distance. People that jogged cautiously to find their feet suddenly dropped a cog and powered ahead. Perhaps they left the cab running outside, because surely they couldn't expect to keep up those strides for the next few hours, especially when the temperature and humidity was only going to rise?

If I've noticed something from my first two events, it's that rain tends to excite people. Or, at the very least, instil a bit of urgency. If you grew up in rainy Britain, then perhaps you'll have memories of when a few spots of rain would appear on your patio, and you could then bet your whole house that moments later you'd hear Mum tumble down the stairs commanding, 'Get the washing in!' Then there's sports day at school, or even playtimes, where a sudden shower would incite mass hysteria of screaming kids rushing to take cover. Our brains must be programmed to seek the fastest exit from any quick downpour, because as the onslaught of rain grew in venom everyone seemed to answer their internal urges to speed up and get home.

I suppose it comes down to one of my favourite sayings: Some people feel the rain, others just get wet. I had read that due to the dreaded wall, the real marathon doesn't start until mile 20. As such, I coached myself through each lap, remembering that pace did not matter one bit, but rather feeling comfortable enough to settle into a rhythm. I didn't mind the rain at all, in fact I was loving the harsh conditions.

This is the kind of challenge I wanted. The sky darkened, the clouds growled, and the rain really chucked it down onto the entirely exposed circuit. The weather was proper giving it the biguns. 'Drink it in, Warren,' I reminded myself knowing that as soon as this spring shower elapsed the summer's heat would soon take over. The agro up in the sky threatened to kick off into a full-blown thunderstorm, until I eyed up clear blue in the far distance beyond the motorway. This divergence from the doomsayers' warning of our live cremations would therefore only be temporary, meaning now was definitely not the time to be skimping at the water stations.

Completing each lap was a true joy early on; wave to Mum and Nan, smile to show them I'm still feeling good, and then fling one band into the giant bin and try not to miss. With each lap my wrist would gradually reclaim its freedom. The rain continued, but blimey was it refreshing! The heavy drops were like a mobile coolant, stopping my temperature gauge from jumping too high.

For a few laps I enjoyed some of the most pleasant miles in my running career so far; the weather was a marvel and the pace felt comfortable. All those tiny niggles and tight, nervous muscles had relaxed into the groove. My mind and body synced up at last, and very gradually, my pace began to rise- *I'm running a marathon!*

Oh yes. Moments like this are special. I savoured the feeling of performing at my maximum potential. Every fibre worked in harmony to guide me through the finale to this great challenge.

It was this feeling from which I derived so much pride, for I had reached what I felt then to be the best version of myself.

I am very glad I savoured the moment on lap 7, completing my fastest lap after a blissful hour in the rain. Do you know why? Because right after that the entire run went completely and utterly tits up. For all that self-appraisal, I would now have to put all the poetry about personal growth to the test as the darkness lifted. Now, the angry clouds had finished pissing all over us and set course for their next part of the country to ruin. A couple of pure white clouds and clear blue skies sat behind the mess, and behind them was the happiest sun you could have ever seen- 27 degrees too happy for my liking.

Oh my gosh I think I'm gonna die

The rain ceased. The temperature crept up, and very quickly the world around us brightened- the same could not be said for my run prospects however, as I was already beginning to feel the effects of the humidity. Lap 7 may have been my quickest time after a smooth shift into a comfortable rhythm, but that rhythm had already collapsed a lap later. Sometimes on a run you can sense the nerves building within, the fear that something is going wrong and won't get any better. With unprecedented levels of humidity, I wondered if I could cope, but the damning truth was that it was already beginning to take its toll. I could drink all the water I wanted and keep taking on gels, but the fact is this scrawny white teenager had met his match against the tropical weather.

Lap 8 was when those nerves started to amplify. With each breath it felt like my lungs were taking on less oxygen, a mix between my throat tightening and the air thinning. Meanwhile, each step felt heavier and heavier as time seemingly slowed. Of course, it wasn't time that was slowing, but me. Unknowingly I had dropped the pace, slowing my stride but disproportionately increasing my air intake. The breaths became heavy. In-in out-out became in-in out-out-out, and then soon in-in out-out-out iiiiin, out-out-out- I couldn't keep up. These worries soon dominated my conscious thoughts. I knew I could keep going- stopping was just a fear- but how long could I keep up this resistance to the heat? I completed the lap with a pained smile and rapidly rising dread; these conditions were only going to get harder.

A couple of laps later and the course was like a desert. The sun has spread its rays as far as the eye could see with temperatures now touching 30 degrees. Not a drop of rain remained on the course. Some camps had set up a garden hose to spray runners as they passed. I made it a must on my mental checklist to free-ride the cooling service each lap in a desperate bid to stay cool- oh how I missed the rain. Taking on water on the back straight always became an urgent priority but drinking from the small plastic cups proved a right faff. I didn't want to stop running, but every time I tried to drink while on the move I'd spill about half of it down me, a quarter would go down the wrong hole, and then the rest would treacle out both sides of my desperate gob. It wasn't working at all; amidst the scorching heat, even carrying around that a water bottle felt like running with a massive dumbbell.

I looked to my wrist which was still full of elastic bands. The bin at the start/finish had bands lying everywhere except inside it, showing off just how many laps other runners had already completed- and obviously how many of them had missed the bin- all while my wrist remained constricted by the rubber chains. With the heat bearing down, no longer did I want to think about how much further I had to go, because I had not even reached the halfway point before my body began urging me to ease off. What's more, the veteran runners sharing this small circuit with me showed no signs of slowing down; many of whom had taken their tops off and continued to power through the thick wall of humidity with no signs of stopping. By this time at Silverstone, I was the one mopping up the lagging 'opposition', but now, I became one of the backmarkers, lapped over and over as the field sped up and I slowed down. No part of my mind could think of pacing any more, now the focus had switched purely to surviving.

'It's getting a little bit hard now!' I chirp to my camp after another lap of almost spontaneously combusting.

'Keep going dear!'

'You're almost halfway!' Mum and Nan replied, now enjoying the gorgeous sun from the side-lines with what I suspected was a

Battenburg to complement their sandwiches. I, meanwhile, pulled out my second gel in desperate hope of it igniting the much-needed spark to rekindle all my lost pace and shoo off the pressing panic to quit.

For an ephemeral moment, the gel kicked in and I recaptured the sensation of running without pain nor panic. I followed it with a generous helping of water which kept me alert throughout the lap. Only until I reached the final section did my body temperature begin creeping up, but at this point I became used to cooling it back down with water. The system appeared to work, but once the gel's brief burst of life died away inside, the fight to stifle an increasingly rising body temperature resumed.

The point of mental crisis where I so desperately wished to stop pricked me earlier and earlier each lap and soon no amount of water seemed capable of quenching my thirst. I reached for the emergency jelly babies, hoping a sugar rush could restart my systems and keep me moving. Opening the bag was such a faff; pulling the right zip required too much hassle- it was complex like simultaneously turning two keys and inputting a secret code just to access the bag of jellies. I'm sure launching a couple of nuclear missiles would have probably been easier. I gulped down a couple and struggled to chew from the sheer dryness of my mouth. The sugar rush never came, and the whole idea proved to be a complete disaster for two reasons.

Firstly, when I reached for a couple of jelly babies from my bum bag, I dropped the entire bag on the floor with a few spilling out. Thinking it would be a lucky excuse to stop, I bent down to pick them up, but as I arched my back and bent my legs, I suddenly realised that my body had aged by about 80 years; every single muscle grouched and stiffened and ached. I felt as if every ligament was on the verge of tearing, every bone near breaking, and every muscle not far from outright exploding. On the way back up my thighs had become so weak and starved of oxygen that I felt like I had just done a full-bodyweight squat.

Secondly, it appeared my stomach had completely given up on digesting anything. A black hole must have formed inside, because no matter what went in nothing seemed to settle. Instead, I carried this heavy, unnerving sensation that suggested the whole gaff could be about to collapse internally. Now at the halfway point, I had slowed to what would normally be considered a light jog, but with the mental and physical agony of a full-blown sprint. Whatever was in my belly, it couldn't digest.

The morning rapidly progressed and the sun ascended higher in the sky. No escape. With each heavy breath I urged myself to relax and to not think about stopping. But easier said than done, right? By simply telling myself to relax and calm down I felt more agitated and helpless to the fact that my mind was hysterically screaming for me to allow a break. The screams had grown so loud and frequent that I could not shield myself from them any longer. I had already slowed to walking pace despite maintaining running strides, but without the strength amidst each helpless breath the pace had completely vanished. I couldn't keep this up much longer. I would either vomit, collapse, or worst of all, suffer jelly legs in front of Mum and Nan and gift them a timeless classic to tell at the Christmas dinner table of how Ellis hilariously fumbled out of his first marathon.

Also, with photographers rampant and the horrifying prospect of me ending this book 'Running for Success' in the back of an ambulance, I had to make a wise call. I decided to take a five-minute walk and let my heartrate slow down. I cannot lie in saying that at the time there was an element of guilt. I didn't want to stop! I didn't want to give in to the easier option! But of course, silly stubbornness is toxic for success. With dehydration kicking in, my heart was essentially ricocheting around my ribcage, such was the immense shift it had to put in. The unnerving fact that marathon runners who push too far in the heat have been known to collapse- or in worst case scenarios, die- meant that walking to calm the internal systems down was definitely the right thing to do. Risking your life for the sake of a bit of self-pride is silly, not to mention dying from your own ego is certainly not an ideal way to go out.

Initially, I felt like it was a weakness to give in to my mind's demands to stop, but then I had to remind myself (not for the first time) to stop being so ridiculous. Just listen to your body and you *will* know. If you have no heart monitor to tell you then use common sense; if you feel like you're about to die, then I needn't tell you that you should probably ease off a bit. At the end of the day, we must not confuse bravery with stupidity; it's better to stop and take in all the oxygen you need in your own time than to collapse and wake up hours later with a mask on to breathe.

I would soon get confirmation of my body's desperate need to slow down- as if it hasn't been blatant enough- when on lap 12 I experienced a bit of a crisis. First came the most excruciating stitch I have ever felt in my whole life to this day. I mentioned black holes before- this was another one, only this time it felt like someone had fired a flipping rocket through my abdomen; was a proper persistent bastard too. No matter how slow I walked, or however hard I gripped the pain, it would not cease biting my abs.

The second problem was my bladder had decided it wanted to offload about 5 litres of hastily consumed water over the past three hours and it would not be made to wait any longer. Thankfully, the course had portable loos easily accessible, so I darted off for a slash at the next opportunity. Now apologies if you're currently drinking your tea, but upon doing my business in the urinal I found that what was coming out wasn't the standard colour, but rather the same colour as the lager I kicked back at the New Year's party with my mates. I saw first-hand the absolute 'mare my kidneys were going through and from then on acknowledged the hard strain my body was under to support me through this. I could only repay it by staying within sensible limits.

Thus, another self-pep talk was required.

'This is a lesson you learnt before and if needs be, one you'll learn again. Let's keep it steady and composed and not overdo it.' In truth, learning not to overdo it is a lesson you may need to hammer into yourself over and over. With a growth mindset, you're constantly looking to break your limits and set new ones, but sometimes at the cost of biting off more than you can chew. Current circumstances required keeping it steady by constantly moving- nothing less, but nothing more either.

To be honest, I did now rue that challenge made to mother nature to give me her worst. It seems she's always got an ace up her sleeve. Nevertheless, I had to press on. Each word came out as a weak groan under heavy huffs and puffs. I thought they were too limp to escape my breath, but one particularly steely man heard my little pep-talk as he went past.

'You alright mate?'

'Yeah, just getting my breath back!'

'Keep going; we're all going through it at the moment, but we've all trained for the distance so we can do this!'

He was right. He looked to be a seasoned marathoner, judging by his running club attire and effortless pace. His words reminded me that I wasn't the only one baking out here. I shared the course with hundreds of other runners also wishing the sun was less hellbent on frying us to a crisp. Every one of us ran under the same sky and despite the gruelling conditions, we soldiered on because every step forward made the finish line that little bit nearer.

Stopping to walk would be okay. In fact, most other runners had done the same. Many of whom began marching to keep their muscles from seizing and to maintain a decent pace. This is in fact a very good strategy and one I highly recommend- it's the middle ground between walking and jogging and the energy used from your arms and legs might just push you to break into a jog and then a run. Regardless of your means of travel, you have to just keep moving, 'one foot in front of the other' as the conventional wisdom states.

Back at base, Mum and Nan had now moved onto a lightly salted packet of crisps.[27] Each lap I returned panting and sweating profusely, but I remained keen to demonstrate that I was no quitter. I did however slightly sense that Nan might appreciate moving out of the sun before long, judging by the deepening shade of red appearing on her legs. The two of them were enjoying a right jolly watching all of us go around, with Mum remarking, 'I feel fitter just by being around all these marathoners!' Glad as I felt that they were enjoying their afternoon in the sun, I figured I ought to get a move on before one of them got sunstroke.

Victory march

On lap 15 I remembered how important it was to stay faithful to the original plan. The goal was to finish- no Ifs nor Buts. It wasn't to run a sub-4 marathon and it wasn't to run without stopping- it was simply to finish. That was what I trained for and originally set out to do, only now midway through the run from hell itself did I fully understand that- better late than never, eh?

---

[27] I must add that in hindsight, I really ought to have taken a pack for the next lap. The reason for this is because during hot weather conditions the body's sodium levels deplete faster with increased sweat. Taking on a bit of salt will bolster those levels, keep your fluids intact, and prevent you from getting dehydrated. Scientists advise taking on sodium when hydrating before the start of a race; to do this there are many sodium tablets available on the market specifically for long distance runners. For more information about the science behind this advice, read: Souza, R. F. d. et al., 2018. Is sodium a good hyperhydration strategy in 10k runners?. *Journal of Human Sport and Exercise*, 13(4), pp. 823-831.

To tell the truth, the dehydration, the dread of at least another hour of running, and the overall feeling that this marathon would never really end threatened to kill my mood and morale because at this stage, my motivation was collapsing. But it didn't. I'm sure you'll remember the reason for this. No longer do we count on motivation to decide whether we act or not. No longer do we allow our mood to decide our judgement and actions. No longer will dread dictate whether we act or not! No thinking, just acting. In my situation, the unmotivated would probably quit and deem the whole exercise a failure. But those with willpower recognise that they are committed to their goals. They realise that commitments must be honoured, and thus each task is completed as a duty, and most importantly, carried out right to the very end.

As I pressed forward for the final 6 miles, I pondered the adult world that I would soon enter. The world for big boys and girls is one full of commitments and obligations. Starting a job, starting a business, buying a house etc., all substantial agreements that to be successful require full dedication. Running this marathon would be the first trial of the mentality needed to be successful in the big ruthless world that awaited. I had conquered my first year of university study, learnt to deal with the social anxiety that crippled me throughout the first term, and now I would conquer the marathon and gain the self-belief that I had the grit and discipline to cope with whatever setbacks life throws.

The final 6 miles were a war, but one which I knew I would win. The stitch bit further into my abs, my throat choked for more oxygen, and my muscles grew heavier and threatened to cramp.

All mere fear mongering at this point because all I needed to do was slow to a walk and allow enough time to lower my heart rate before attempting to run again. Either way, I was moving forward. Because of that, every step taken, whether by walking or running, was equally successful.

On lap 18 I remembered my reasons for taking up this journey. I remembered the dark place I was in when I made the decision to change for the better. I no longer wanted to be lonely, nor did I want to feel lost anymore. I wanted a reason to attack each day and I wanted a passion again. I knew I couldn't cling to the past any longer, because life moves quick at university. I knew I had to reinvent myself because I didn't want to be a failure. I didn't want to put all the years of hard work to be the first person in my family to reach university to waste. I wanted to be happy in my new environment. I wanted to feel comfortable with my identity. I wanted to make Mum and Nan proud. I wanted to make my friends proud. And I wanted to make myself proud. All my life I've known of my capabilities but never followed my creative and sporting passions enough to see success, all due to a lack of self-belief. I wanted to change that. I wanted to be better.

With this in mind, I pushed hard, and ran. I ran with the thought of every setback, from childhood to now, that led me to this very moment. I reflected on every time I thought of myself in a negative way and remembered believing so many negative and horrible things about myself. All those negative perceptions from the past became fuel for the fire that burned away the doubts and fears of who I am now. This was the lap where I proved to myself that I was strong, capable, and most of all, worthy. I became encapsulated by a second wind that pushed me to complete the entire lap without stopping to walk, something I hadn't done in hours. It was a very personal lap.

That rush of emotion and energy then completely vanished at the beginning of lap 19. I sensed that the previous lap's second wind had a somewhat therapeutic purpose, as if to finally rid me of the mental chains that previously held me back all these years. Could've done with it lasting a bit longer to be honest. Oh well. I knew I had to keep surging ahead; I knew I had to fight to the finish because the longer I took the more Mum and Nan would fry in the sun. I couldn't keep the two lobsters waiting much more; this was not just for me, but for them as well. If ever I needed another reason to keep pressing, then that was it.

Lap 19 took significantly longer to complete, but the encouragement from the fact I was so close to finishing cheered louder than the concerns for my condition, which no longer bothered me. With many other runners already finished, I would catch the odd glimpse of depleted bodies slumped in folding chairs. I noticed that they were slumped perhaps not from fatigue, but from the humungous medal hanging from their necks. Woah- the medal on offer for completing this marathon was ridiculously big! I would say it looked about 5x the size of my Silverstone medal and it was specially designed for this very event, with a Pocahontas-themed design that included three metal feathers dangling from the bottom. It even had the event date, name, and location escribed too. *I had to have it.* I couldn't wait to have that gorgeous bit of bling dangling from my neck and thus charged ahead to the 20th and final lap.

As I passed Mum and Nan for the penultimate time, they gave a huge cheer as I tossed my bum bag back to base- don't need that anymore! Then, as I crossed the start/finish to begin my last circulation I flung the final elastic band into the bin- my wrist was finally liberated! Just one final push. Any attempt to try and run after 5 hours out in the sun now proved futile- but whatever- let's march towards victory!

Other runners and family spectators cheered me on from the sides, marshals also energetically applauded me to the finish- apart from one who told me I should train a bit harder next time, but given that he wasn't out there running himself I had good reason to believe his own advice probably hadn't gone too well for him.

I progressed through the final lap by walking, as every attempt to run was met with threats of full body cramping. Absolutely *everything* ached. But, when I saw that final straight to the line, I knew there could only be one way to finish. I set my sights at the special coned off lane for finishers and pressed forward into a sprint to utilise every last remaining bit of energy, to empty the tank fully, and to finish my first ever marathon victorious.

As I drove my arms and galloped with both legs, Mum rose to try and immortalise the moment on video, almost completely missing me. She said I was too fast to capture on camera, but we all know it was because she couldn't get the camera app to load in time. When watching it back, I look desperately slow, but at the time I felt like I was about to break the sound barrier.

Once the finish line came into sight none of my pains from the whole morning could touch me anymore. It was over. I finally completed the marathon after 5 hours 10 minutes and 40 seconds of fighting with myself and the elements. All of us out there experienced tropical downpours, intense humidity, and temperatures reaching 30 degrees- I doubt I'll run through tougher conditions in the UK again.

As I left the circuit an official greeted me with the gigantic medal. The moment I had been waiting for was perfectly sweet- what an incredible piece of craftmanship and a perfect memento for this hard-fought achievement. I hobbled off to see Mum and Nan, realising that that final charge to the line had upset my Achilles tendon, but who cares at this point? I would probably be immobile the next morning anyway.

Sitting down after 5 hours on my feet was the ultimate relief, right after I managed to slowly lower myself down to avoid cramp. Speaking of which, I watched the rest of the runners still out there, most of them walking or hobbling, and one of them stopping in agony right in front of us as his calf cramped up. Boy did I feel glad that was no longer me.

Looking around at the other finishers, I saw that the majority of them were standing in large groups and chattering away about their races. They all appeared to be close chums and to hazard a guess, most of those 100 marathons each of them had ran had probably been completed together in events much like this one. The group who organised the race seemed to hold many marathons and running events on a frequent basis around the whole country. So for many of the regulars, these events were more than just a running challenge, they were also social gatherings. Watching them banter away opened up my mind to the opposite of the large-scale marathon events. These smaller, more local gatherings seem to provide a great opportunity for mates to get together, complete a marathon, and then indulge in as much chocolate and beer as they could handle, all while sporting their massive, custom-designed medals. It looked like a real fun lifestyle.

After taking my recovery protein shake and changing into some comfy clothes, I limped with Mum and Nan back to the car, proudly displaying my marathon medal, and probably chatting absolute rubbish as the runner's high set in; after such an intense struggle, this euphoric relief felt more akin to being sedated. I could cry tears of joy that those painstaking 5 hours were over.

Back at Nan's we celebrated the day with a feast consisting of the most gorgeous, hard-earned Chinese takeaway of my entire life. Having burnt upwards of 2,500 calories during the marathon, I would feel no guilt in eating whatever I fancied for the next few days, or months.

You may have expected this chapter to chronicle my epic survival of the heat where I ran on defiantly towards the finish. That didn't happen, but the run was still just as successful- if not more- than if it did. In fact, I felt glad that I had the toughest possible introduction to marathon running. I cursed the weather at the time, but looking back, if I could complete a marathon in those conditions, I could complete any marathon around the entire world.

For the whole afternoon, I put my feet up and chilled: Chinese takeaway on my lap, Formula 1 on the telly- pure bliss. I could hardly move from the sofa, such was the stiffness- no amount of WD40 could get me going again at this point. At night, I expected to fall asleep instantly and experience the greatest slumber ever recorded in human history, but truth be told I repeatedly tossed and turned and felt very restless. Perhaps my mind was still in overdrive from being in survival mode for a prolonged period. Eventually, I drifted off and slept like a log for the next nine hours.

When I awoke the next morning, my whole body throbbed. Every movement occurred in painful, aching slow-motion. I felt like I could have done with another nine hours. Today would definitely be the least productive day of the year (as if I cared!). It's safe to say the marathon and those conditions absolutely battered me. And, as I emerged from my bed and gazed at the huge medal on the bedside table, only one thought danced around my mind: I can't wait to do that all again.

Chapter 12
Post-marathon:
What you should be aware of

Now what? That's a question I never imagined asking myself. After months of focussing all my efforts on my running and university goals, I now stood on the other side of their success. Beyond the big goal of beating the marathon and acing my exams lied a completely unknown path, one I had not given any thought towards whatsoever.

Since January, I religiously followed my study and running plans to organise my daily life. Each day was packed with purpose and weaved in nicely towards the long-term goal. We know now all the benefits that followed and we know that it was a life-changing experience. Having such a strong sense of purpose fuelled me to continue those hard efforts throughout the five months. For almost half a year, I disciplined myself to focus solely on two things each day: the next study topic and the next run.

Sure, avoiding late night socials and waking up way too early on a Sunday for long runs that would last well into the afternoon didn't allow much leeway for the ravish and exciting lifestyle a 19-year-old lad like me could have been living. But the truth is, I quickly found myself thriving off that sense of duty. I liked having to organise my life around running; it felt like the sexier alternative to organising everything entirely around study.

Of course, there were times when I wished I could return to my laid back and inconsequential life prior to university, simply because it was easier and involved less responsibility. But we all look back and wish we were kids sometimes. It's not easy growing up. But the fact that this journey was so hard with the learning curve so steep is what made it worthwhile. Running and training for a marathon expanded my comfort zone so I could change for the better- after all, pressure creates diamonds.

Throughout the process and even when I hit rock-bottom during my injury periods, I unknowingly appreciated all the anxieties and fears and doubts that epitomised the journey. After all, they gave me purpose, and that was the one thing I sought the most when I decided to become a runner. It was only until the celebrations had finished and the runner's high faded did I realise that in a strange way I actually missed those doubts and fears.

POST-MARATHON: WHAT YOU SHOULD BE AWARE OF

Crossing the finish line to complete my first marathon truly felt like one of the greatest personal accomplishments- a real year-defining moment. Afterwards, I completed and passed my final exams to wrap up my first year at university. All the intense flashcard-making paid off in tremendous style- first class honours in my first year. Before I knew it, I was packing my belongings to move out of my halls room and boarding the train back home to the quiet countryside for the summer break. The year was over.

When I returned home, I fully expected to enjoy an entire summer of living life at a more relaxed pace and not fretting about study, about running, or about remaining faithful to my daily regime. I thought taking a break from deadlines and targets would prove a pleasant change. And it did- for about three days.

I very quickly started to wonder, 'What shall I do now?' Having taken adequate time- about a fortnight- to let my body heal from the marathon, I could return to running again, and sure, a couple of easy runs back home made me feel good for a while. But it didn't fix the underlying issue: I no longer had anything exciting to look forward to.

It then quickly became apparent that every day had become rather bland. No longer was there a voice in the back of my mind yelling, 'You've got to get this done!', and no longer did I have an important reason to spring out of bed early in the morning and get cracking on the day's work. Life had completely stopped. What was there left to do now that the journey had seemingly ended? Panic set in when I caught my mindset quickly reverting back to the pre-running slump. Suddenly, all that willpower I built to overcome my problems no longer had any use because every day had now become easy and insignificant. I soon found myself spending longer and longer lying on top of my bed, staring at the ceiling each evening. I felt so empty.

The post-marathon life offered little excitement. It no longer mattered if I accomplished my tasks during the day, because there were no tasks. I became indifferent to how I spent the whole summer. Oh to be spoilt with free time; I could watch the films and play the video games that I so wished I had the time for during the five-month grind, but I didn't want to do anything. I didn't even want to see my friends. I became indifferent to every daily choice and stopped caring altogether because nothing seemed worthwhile from my point of view. This of course, was quite an extreme reaction, the opposite extreme to the huge lifestyle change made back at the beginning of the year.

In situations like this, you feel depressed because you think you should be happy at that point. You feel angry at yourself for not being grateful and satisfied that all the hard work had paid off. *Why do I feel this way? Have I done something wrong? What's wrong with me?* It's all so horribly confusing. I thought I had grown and developed into a proper functioning adult. But now I couldn't even get out of bed in the mornings because the basic desire to do so had become strangely absent.

The reason I include this epilogue as an entire chapter is because what I experienced in the month following the completion of my first marathon is something you too may very well have to come to grips with following the completion of a personal goal. These emotions have the potential to consume you after any big achievement, whether it be graduation, the completion of a big project, or the purchase of a dream home to name a few examples. Retirement too springs to mind- why do so many people feel lost after retiring and desperately seek to reinstate value into their new lifestyle? Every scenario begs the question: Why do we feel depressed after a big achievement? The obvious answer is that the grand journey is over and now life's at a standstill- *I've worked so hard to get to the point where I have seemingly everything I wanted- now what?* But, it's one thing to feel a bit down after a big celebratory period of your accomplishment and another for those blues to develop into depression.

This post-achievement slump is a universally recognised phenomenon, one particularly well documented in marathon runners, so much so that it has its own name in the running community: 'post-marathon blues'. This state of mind can vary in severity from feeling down for a few days to falling into a depressed rut.

After my marathon I bordered on the latter- I can tell you from first-hand experience that it is a horrible feeling. If, like me, you started running to make a positive change in your life, you will be overcome with guilt upon the dreaded realisation that you now feel as if you're back to square one.

You may worry that you have become numb to running's positive effects on you. I want to assert that that is not the case. Instead, it is a signal to set your sights towards the future again.

Preventing the post-marathon blues

Can the post-marathon blues be prevented? Yes- but it requires forward-planning that you could be forgiven for not considering when you started your running journey. When I planned for the big event, I saw the marathon as the huge final battle standing in the way of completion. It sounds funny, but I really did not envision what life would be like beyond that point- I just never thought that far ahead.

When I was right in the middle of training, I dared not look beyond the marathon at the risk of becoming complacent. If we take an even further step back from when the marathon was the long-term goal, we now realise that in the context of our whole lives, the marathon is actually a short-term goal.[28] As such, by only looking towards the marathon (and no further) we were deriving purely instant gratification, rather than the deferred gratification it felt like at the time. I use this comparison because training for a specific goal is relevant and important only up to a certain point, whereas looking after our mental health is a life-long matter.

To avoid running yourself into a rut then, you may think about developing a plan or a new goal for after your event before you've even begun training for it. Ask yourself, where does this goal fit into my overall development? What will it enable me to do once it's finished? Remember that questions such as, 'How much weight do I want to lose?', 'What is my target time?', and 'How do I want to feel about myself afterwards?' will probably only provide

---

[28] The marathon is just one example; any goal can apply to this matter.

answers that are relevant specifically to the short-term aftermath of your success. It is important to think of how this journey will set you up for bigger and better things; there has to be something else to look forward to, or at the very least, something you gain from the journey that you can keep with you.

Too often for runners who have successfully achieved their end goal do they lose their motivation to continue the sport and, in many instances, quit altogether. This is one of the particular situations where willpower cannot help you, because what do you have to will yourself on towards? You are no longer bound to any commitment and thus have nothing to measure your success by.

Before my full marathon- which took place on a small course with many local regulars who all knew each other- I had only known the idea of the big events like the London Marathon. I used to think that's what all runners aimed for. When tuning in to watch the event on telly, it appeared everyone had their own personal story for challenging the distance, with most participating for a charity that complements their cause. For a lot of the participants in these large-scale events, the completion of the 26.2 miles marks not just the end of their marathon journey, but their running career as a whole, because many people tackle the event for the sake of raising money and to prove to themselves that they can do it. I personally find that ending it there is a bit of a shame, because as my entire journey up to this point has shown, there's so much more to simply completing the marathon.

When I looked back at the past five months, I viewed the experience not as a sensational once-in-a-life time journey, but as something that could be repeated year after year, aiming just a little bit higher each time. I knew full well that the next three years of my life would be dominated by intense study and exams and viewed marathon training as the ideal complement to achieve academic success.

I realised that like running, to get that first-class honours required long-term planning, diligent dedication, and willpower to be successful. Therefore, it made sense to continue the running journey. I vowed to train and run a marathon every year thereafter as a lifetime goal for continued and sustained success. To keep the journey fresh, I would aim to beat my personal best time on each attempt. Following the extraordinary weather of this year's marathon, I already felt eager to see how much time I could make up next year. By making marathon training an integral part of not just my daily routine, but my yearly one as well, I always had something up ahead to look forward to.

This was just the first measure taken to ensure that I didn't fall into a trench of my own bewilderment again. But what about when you're in the thick of the post-marathon blues? How did I get out of my summer depression? Fortunately, these emotions can be easily conquered through a few key steps. Should you ever find yourself in this position, then there are a few practical solutions to help you get back on your feet.

How to escape the rut

Regardless of what you plan to do in the future, at the goal's end you should take time to review the entire process. Look back on what went well, what could have been improved, and most importantly what you have gained from the whole experience. While the past five months may have felt long and enduring at times, twenty years into the future all the pain and anguish and possibly even the positives may become a faded memory.

Think back briefly to some of the most challenging periods of your life. You may notice you've forgotten a lot about them. One example is school exams; I remember the long hours after school, the constant angst, and the sleepless nights dreading the next day during my GCSEs. Many of my peers experienced the same stress, but years on view that bleak winter through nostalgia goggles- yes, we had some of the best times, but school certainly wasn't without its dark days. Now think of the positive bits of your past which helped you grow and develop new skills. What about that self-help book you read? Or the online course you took? Be honest, how well do you remember what you learnt? Do you still make use of those skills?

The chances are the worthwhile investments of time, money, and energy you made in the past may still be nestled in your noggin somewhere but are at large untouched and almost entirely forgotten. Or maybe this isn't making sense to read, and I just happen to clumsily forget each new skill I set out to learn. The key point is that as humans, we often forget and move on in our lives without properly learning the key lessons. We usually only learn after repeatedly making the same mistakes- as proven with my injury woes back in chapter 6. Our personal development doesn't have to be that inefficient though. By taking the time to look back in detail how our experiments and endeavours panned out, we dissect each positive and negative and find out what made us successful, and what's going to make us even more well off next time we strive to achieve.

When carrying out this analysis, it helps to have your training programme well documented in a running log. In my case, I kept a Word document recording all my weekly mileage and session times with a few extra notes, alongside a WordPress blog that gave a subjective review of how training was unfolding as it happened. I also got the joy of looking back on my blog posts from the height of my injury crises and revelling in the fact that I was no longer trapped in bed with a stack of oven chips on my ankle. With this quantitative and qualitative data, I could practically create a line graph that illustrated the relationship between my mileage and intensity levels with various different variables such as mental wellbeing, physical energy levels, and perceived productivity.

One finding was that all three of those subjective factors dipped towards the end of term at university. While burnout became an increasing risk towards the end of term, my marathon training intensity retained its gradual rise. I originally made this decision to ensure I could complete the minimum mileage required for my events, even if it meant skipping the 'de-load'[29]

---

[29] 'De-load' weeks, like the taper, involve running significantly lower mileage to allow the body to recover from a gradual increase in training

weeks on my plan. My conclusion from this finding was that running performance is lowered while risk of injury increases during busy periods towards the end of the university term. Therefore, it would be a wise move in the future to arrange my de-load weeks towards the end of term, to allow my body to heal while I hit the books and get those papers submitted.

This was just one finding of many which put me in good stead and simultaneously built up anticipation for future running events. Other findings included a more personalised nutrition strategy, preferences for session length, and how many rest days taken between runs. Thanks to all this analysis and pointers for the future, I could begin crafting a new and improved marathon training plan personalised for my capabilities before I had even begun the search for next year's event.

Next involves planning for what lies directly ahead. We have already discussed framing the running journey in terms of its long-term standing within our lives, but now we need to look at the short-term picture. Because obviously, if you're feeling blue following a marathon, fixing next year isn't necessarily going to improve next week. The main takeaway here is finding smaller, but still valuable goals with regards to running. For non-running endeavours you can go crazy and dive into anything you like, but with running I advise against launching a new marathon training programme simply because you probably want to give your body a rest- remember, you've probably already forgotten the pain of

---

intensity. On many standard marathon training plans, de-load weeks are planned for weeks 5 and 10.

training and the day itself (it only took me one night), so let's not go and shatter an ankle through over-enthusiastically initiating the hunt for the next PB.

So, what constitutes 'small' running goals? From my experience, that would be anything from aiming to run a certain number of times during a week, all the way up to attempting a 10K. This is based off the fact that in my situation, I had the whole summer with the same hot weather that tried to kill me during the marathon and an intention to not get unnecessarily injured. Essentially, anything that you can write a small plan for- or even just a solid mental note- will shift you back into that sense of routine, thus straightening you out of the slump while also maintaining your physical fitness.

Throughout the summer months I thus decided to pursue several smaller goals to keep my running fresh and exciting. One of those included spending ten weeks attempting to bring down my 5K times while also forcing myself to learn how to cope in hot weather. I also tried to settle into the routine of maintaining a weekly base mileage of roughly 15-20 miles every week, so that eventually when I started my next full marathon training programme I would have a solid foundation of fitness to improve performance and reduce injury risk.

Remember that running is possible wherever you are in the world- it's always there for you. When I went to Poland to teach English that summer, running kept me fit, allowed me to explore the forests beyond Warsaw, and kept my head sane after spending

POST-MARATHON: WHAT YOU SHOULD BE AWARE OF

a month surrounded by over 150 kids. Sometimes, you don't even need a running goal, sometimes you just need an outlet.

However you decide to live your life following the conclusion of a running journey, I urge you to not let the completion of a long-term goal or any blues that follow it convince you to quit running altogether. Never forget the highs and lows of your running journey, for it will have no doubt taught you important things about yourself and life in general that will prove valuable lessons later down the line.

To run is to explore everchanging limits within yourself, a means of pushing you to new levels no matter what stage you are at in life. Many people will lecture you about how life is short, but as a runner you must understand that our lives are long. This is because we never stop growing; there is always enough time in our lives to learn and evolve into better and more capable human beings through exercise. After all, it's a marathon, not a sprint.

Chapter 13
Onto the next challenge

And so, our first running journey ends and the next adventure- one that spans the whole of our lifetimes- begins. When I set out on that first run on New Year's Day, I had two feelings: a desperate desire to prove to myself that I could overcome my troubles at university and a proper stabbing stitch. Originally, I hoped that by the end of training and attempting a marathon, I would conquer what I considered my weaknesses.

In the end, I gained so much more than I could have ever anticipated. Looking back on my first marathon and my first year at university, I learnt that while the result is obviously important, the real value is in the journey. By plugging away each day and gaining incrementally each time, the goals were essentially already achieved by the time the big tests had arrived. I knew I could run a marathon as early as the day I completed training, and I knew I could get the top grade in my exams as early as the revision lectures, where suddenly, the quiet awkward kid in the back row had moved to the front, and was now confidently contributing correct answers in front of an unusually muted class.

I knew I could get to the end of any task with willpower, the central concept within this book that asserts that motivation is too unreliable in achieving our aims; instead, willpower, which is the tenacity to carry out every task as a duty to its end, is a much more effective driving force for it does not rely on thoughts or feelings, just acting. Of course, the way to build up willpower was through running itself.

Thanks to running, I learnt to thrive off a growth mindset to push through each task. I now had the faith in my will to work and succeed that if I were to plan for success, I would be confident in disciplining myself towards that goal. With this self-belief, all I had to do was plan and work and most important of all, learn- no longer would there be any failures, just learning experiences for the next attempt.

I also realised that no amount of natural talent is useful without hard work and a tenacious attitude. Frankly speaking, I believe this was one of the primary reasons why I ultimately succeeded in my first year and so many failed and dropped out. In fact, four years later I was the only BA Japanese and Economics graduate in my university's class of 2020.

It certainly took a while to adjust to life in the big city of London, culturally so different to the small Medway towns where I grew up. On the university campus I also felt very much an outcast- an introvert in an extrovert's paradise. For a whole term I lamented the differences, became horribly homesick, and eventually depressed. I dreaded the prospect of continuing the misery for another three-and-a-half years.

But the thing is, the world around you is probably never going to change the way you want. You can of course change courses, move cities, move to different universities, colleges, or jobs, but if you're clinging onto a past or a feeling that cannot be relived then you're setting yourself up for endless disappointment. At some point you have to start taking responsibility for why you're dissatisfied, otherwise, you may well end up like the majority of unhappy people out there who always find something or someone other than themselves to blame. As Einstein said, the definition of insanity is trying the same thing over and over and expecting different results.

So, as this book hopes to exemplify, rather than changing the environment around you, it is so much easier to change yourself. As humans we seek novelty and excitement, but we cannot find that in a limited comfort zone, within our bubble of beliefs and values. We have to reinvent ourselves following big change and adapt to our new environments for the sake of both surviving *and* thriving- that's how our ancestors got here, times change but the game remains the same.

Sometimes, redirecting the problem towards ourselves can be difficult and even if we have been affected by unavoidable circumstances that weren't our fault, taking full responsibility for how we want to feel about ourselves in the future may well pave the way for the solution. In my case, I targeted my clear weak points that had plagued me through my past endeavours and sought to not necessarily correct them but face them head on. In doing so I ventured into the enchanting world of running and haven't looked back since.

This book has shown what running has done for me and what it can so easily do for you. My story is just one among countless others of ordinary people who have dragged themselves out of difficult times in their lives and gone onto turn everything around in extraordinary ways. Running can be not just a life-changer, but a lifesaver too. The empowerment the sport gives to our self-esteem and the positive impact on our mental health is something I feel we can all benefit from. It has been my goal since that first marathon to spread the powerful life tool that is running in ways that can be applied to all of us- I hope this book has provided an ample start to that goal.

Following the summer of 2017, I returned to university for my second year knowing full well this could be the toughest 12 months of my whole degree. Money was low- actually let me rephrase that, I couldn't afford to live in London, even a parking space was too expensive, so I would have to commute from home for 4 hours each day, driving to the station, boarding the train, and then taking the tube to university. I had three times more classes during the week and worst of all, this would be the year the economics department forced me to take pure maths- the old enemy. I thought I had escaped from regular numerical headaches after GCSEs, yet suddenly found myself staring blankly at Lagrange multipliers and calculus.

But, even with old weaknesses remerging, running was once again both a reminder and a supporter through my attempts at tackling the seemingly impossible. The story of my second year is one for another day, for it went on to encompass challenges and tough moments that I would wish no other human to ever experience. Let's just say for the time being that by the end, I was gladder than ever to have discovered running during my first year.

To this day, the goal of running a marathon each year stands as strong as ever. In fact, my zeal for the sport has already taken me beyond that goal as of 2020. Since my first year of university, I have run ten marathons, including one in Japan and seven in the midst of a global pandemic. Again, those are all stories for another day, but for the time being I will leave you with a brief summary of the key lessons learned in this one. Here are ten tips running has taught me which I hope will spur you onto continued success in all areas of life:

10 Tips from Running for Success

1. Change starts with you. Consider your weaknesses and think honestly about why you have not overcome them yet.

2. Use your inspirations and reasons to power you through tough points.

3. Set clear attainable goals and break down the small tasks required to accomplish them over the long-term.

4. Your goals are your business. It is not necessary for others to know your every intention, and the absence of external pressure from keeping them private may benefit you.

5. Respect your body's limits and never overexert yourself. Saving yourself for tomorrow is better than being side-lined for all of next month.

6. Learn your lessons otherwise you will inevitably repeat the same mistakes.

7. When low on motivation, stop relying on thoughts and feelings to act, for they will only persuade you to back out and quit. Instead, use willpower to carry out your commitments and *just act*.

8. Your personal journey doesn't have to just be about you; charity offers the chance to make a profound difference for those less fortunate while also galvanising the support of your friends, family, and colleagues.

9. Life is long. Always be open to learn and grow further- we have plenty of time to learn new skills and develop existing ones.

10. Always respect the scale of your challenge. In the case of the marathon, always respect the 26.2-mile distance or risk coming a cropper and looking like a right muppet.

With these tips and the story of this book, perhaps your first venture into running will be less of a topsy-turvy ride. But that doesn't mean it'll be a smooth one by any means. Now, the most important next step is to get out there and start taking action for yourself. Cease listening to the naysayers of running who quit after their first setback, and know that if you do encounter a tough period, then perceive it as a trial gifted to you with the prospect of becoming stronger and more capable by the end. Embrace the lows as much as you enjoy the highs and watch the transformation into a better you take place.

Let this be the day you start throwing away excuses and ignore the volatility of motivation; from now on we plan our goals and use willpower to execute them. From now on we use running as a trusty tool to pick us up when we need a lift and to keep us ambitious and resolute for whatever the future throws at us. In doing so, I believe we can all become happier, healthier, and more prosperous human beings. Take that courageous step forward today, ride the setbacks, and conquer your weaknesses through running.

I wish you the very best of luck in your endeavours and hope running yields the same life-changing benefits for you.

It's not going to be easy, but it will definitely be worth it.

Please leave a review!

Thank you so much for reading.

If you enjoyed this book or have any feedback you would like to share, I would really appreciate it if you could leave a review.

And, if you have any questions or would like to get in touch, then please contact me at elliswarren.com!

To keep up to date with new releases and read my new books for FREE, sign up to my mailing list, also at elliswarren.com!

About Ellis Warren

Ellis Warren's aim is to create works that entertain and inspire. Since graduating with First Class Honours in Japanese and Economics, he hopes to continue his love of writing alongside his professional life from Tokyo, Japan.

An avid runner since 2017, Ellis has completed 10 marathons in 3 years and hopes to use the experience to encourage others to enjoy a similar transformation as he did. He is also a campaigner for mental health awareness, and in 2020, ran 5 marathons in 2 months to raise awareness for suicide prevention.

Ellis' dream is to become an indie author. After the release of *Running for Success*, he hopes to continue releasing both fiction and non-fiction works in the future. You can support his efforts and find out about future releases through elliswarren.com.

Printed in Great Britain
by Amazon